FLIP FLOP FLY BALL
AN INFOGRAPHIC BASEBALL ADVENTURE

CRAIG ROBINSON

BLOOMSBURY
NEW YORK · BERLIN · LONDON · SYDNEY

Published by Bloomsbury USA, New York

All papers used by Bloomsbury USA are natural, recyclable products made from wood grown in well-managed
forests. The manufacturing processes conform to the environmental regulations of the country of origin.

LIBRARY OF CONGRESS CATALOGING-IN-PUBLICATION DATA

Robinson, Craig, 1970–
Flip flop fly ball : an infographic baseball adventure / Craig Robinson.
p. cm.
ISBN: 978-1-60819-269-4
1. Baseball—United States—Anecdotes. 2. Baseball fields—United States—Anecdotes. 3. Robinson, Craig, 1970—Anecdotes. I. Title.
GV867.R542 2011
796.357—dc22
2010035130

First U.S. Edition 2011

1 3 5 7 9 10 8 6 4 2

Designed by Elizabeth Van Itallie
Printed in China by South China Printing Company, Dongguan, Guangdong

FOR JOHN BASSETT,
AS GOOD A FRIEND AS ONE
COULD EVER HOPE FOR

FLIP FLOP FOREWORD

BY ROB NEYER

I have been following baseball, somewhat obsessively, for thirty-five years.

I have been studying baseball, somewhat obsessively, for twenty-five years.

I have been writing about baseball, somewhat professionally, for twenty years.

I'm not foolish enough to think I know everything worth knowing about baseball. I'm not foolish enough to think I know a *thousandth* of everything there is to know about baseball. The more I learn, though, the harder it becomes to find new *ways* of learning. I've read the books. I've watched the games. I've listened to so many ex-players during so many hundreds of games on TV that I probably know Joe Morgan and Hawk Harrelson and Mike Krukow better than their own children know them. Every winter I used to rip open packs of baseball cards to see the new designs, admire the photos, pore over the numbers on the backs. Every spring I used to haunt the magazine racks and grab the newest magazines previewing the coming baseball seasons. I don't do those things anymore. Those roses have lost their bloom. For me, anyway.

I was going to quote Jacques Barzun—a Frenchman who came to America for school, fell in love with baseball, and never left—but I've always considered his famous line about baseball* a bit too facile, and it's become only more facile when repeated for decades. But Barzun's mind was—and still is, apparently, even at 103—so active, one wishes that among his forty-some books was one about baseball. Barzun must have seen things, when he watched baseball, that most of us just don't see. Because we were born with it, and we don't think about it any more than

we think about breathing or listening to Top 40 songs. Craig Robinson, born in England and living in Germany, is a Barzun for our times. It's not so odd to me that he sees things I don't see; there are a lot of things I don't see. What's odd to me is that Craig sees things that nobody else sees.

As I write this, early in October, in the last twenty-four some odd hours Roy Halladay and Tim Lincecum pitched two of the greatest games in baseball's postseason history. After both games, I cobbled some thoughts together for publication because . . . well, because that's what I do. It's my vocation and, at least to a point, my avocation as well. I'm sure my cobblings weren't as good as some of the other dozens of reactions; I hope they were better than at least a few.

It's not easy. Lately we call it blogging, but baseball writers have been doing essentially what I do for well more than a century. It's difficult—and I'm not complaining, because I'm paid decent money to accomplish the difficult—to see things in baseball, even things like Roy Halladay throwing a no-hitter in the playoffs, in something like a different light.

Granted, I don't have much of an imagination. No, really, I don't. People who don't write for a living figure that writers have fantastic imaginations. Well, we don't. Not all of us, anyway. Sure, I can imagine the hell out of things when I'm unconscious; I've got a dream journal as proof. But the second my eyes open in the morning, I'm just another literal-minded schmuck with a day job who likes to go to the movies.

A few years ago I wrote a book with Bill James. The heart of the book was a compendium of (among other things) the pitches thrown by hundreds of notable pitchers. But what constitutes *notable*, exactly? Well, there's really nothing exact about notable; my notable's

* "Whoever wants to know the heart and mind of America had better learn baseball, the rules and realities of the game."

different from your notable, which is different from the next guy's notable. Still, I obsessed about what that word might mean to anyone who happened to pick up the book. We included pitchers who threw no-hitters, and pitchers who won awards, and as many Negro Leagues pitchers as we could find. We included pitchers who threw a certain number of innings, and anybody else everyone's heard of even if they're not sure why.

Still, I obsessed. And I e-mailed a bunch of people with imaginations better than mine and I just asked them: "Who should be in this book that I might not already have thought of?"

A friend who writes for television responded with two words: *fictional characters*.

I could have done nothing but think about the meaning of *notable* for the rest of my life and not thought of that. But of course it was brilliant. I just needed those two words, that single burst of imagination, and I was off to the races. My single favorite bit in the book is the entry for Charlie Brown, in which we learn his theoretical repertoire of pitches (1. Fastball; 2. Curveball; 3. Drop Ball; 4. Knuckleball) and his actual repertoire (1. Straight Ball; 2. Straight Ball; 3. Straight Ball; 4. Straight Ball). We also learn that Brown stood four feet two inches, weighed eighty-seven pounds, and "gave up an unusual number of line drives up the middle."

That's good stuff, I think. But I can take but little credit, as I was merely a medium for the imaginations of Charles Schulz and my friend the television writer. I needed that little push, that spark of imagination, and then it was easy: I could make up a long list of fictional pitchers that I knew, from Charlie Brown to Sidd Finch and Henry Wiggen.

Last spring Dallas Braden caused a stir by dressing down Alex Rodriguez during a game in Oakland, after Rodriguez had the temerity to tread on the pitcher's mound while Braden was working. I had no idea what to do about this (aside from my usual cobblings). But I'd been following Craig Robinson for long enough to think that *he* might have an idea. So I e-mailed him. I didn't have anything to offer, other than a suggestion that he engage *his* imagination, *his* talents, *his* offbeat way of looking at baseball, and maybe come up with something nobody else would.

Which of course is exactly what he did. Within a few hours, Craig devised my single favorite invention of the entire 2010 baseball season: *Bradenia*, an autonomous pitching-mound-shaped region of Oakland Athletica. (A few weeks later, when Braden improbably pitched a perfect game, Craig updated his map of Oakland Athletica to include Bradenia's annexed territory of Firstbase Land.)

There are dozens (okay, hundreds) of people who can do what I do. Some a little better, some (I hope) a little worse. But as near as I can tell, there's just one man on the planet who can do what Craig Robinson can do. This might seem strange to you. I'll bet ol' Jacques Barzun would get it, though. And I'll bet you'll get it, too, as you turn these pages and read the words and look at Craig's stunning graphics, both beautiful and insightful. I don't know that any of us can see baseball quite the way Craig sees it. But I doubt, after reading this book, that any of us will see it the same way we saw it before.

Now if you'll excuse me, I have to go see what the Englishman in Germany / Canada / Mexico / wherever he is thinks about Roy Halladay and Tim Lincecum.

FALLING IN LOVE

October 17, 1978. Los Angeles, California. Top of the seventh. Reggie Jackson hits Bob Welch's first pitch out of the park. Eight years old, listening to Bill White on the radio, fighting the urge to sleep, I celebrate quietly underneath the bedsheets. The Yankees had just gone up 7–2 against the Dodgers. The Yankees were nine outs away from a second straight World Series win. This sort of childhood memory is probably the way a book about baseball is supposed to begin. It's only a hazy memory, propped up by shoeboxes full of bleached-out colors in Polaroid photographs and Super 8 film. Photos of me in my Little League uniform, in my bedroom beneath a Don Mattingly poster, in the bleachers with my dad. I could go on for paragraphs describing my father's fastball (not that fast really, but it seemed like Nolan Ryan's when I was a kid). I could keep going on about walking up the ramps at Yankee Stadium and the joy of seeing the field for the first time, seeing the vast outfield, grass the greenest of greens that could ever be. And I could fast-forward to regretting throwing out my baseball cards, regretting the years I strayed from baseball, the years when girls and beer took baseball's place at the top of the *Billboard* Hot 100 of my life.

But none of that is true.

On October 17, 1978, as a child in Lincoln, England, I had no idea what baseball was. Even if I had known what baseball was, British television or radio never mentioned it, and the *Lincolnshire Echo* didn't run the box scores. I certainly couldn't play it at school or with my mates.

For many October seventeenths to follow, I continued not to care about baseball. Actually, "care" is the

A visual metaphor for what it's like being a baseball fan in a country where baseball is not popular: you have to take whatever you can get. Every element of the collage is made up from photographs taken in Berlin.

wrong word: baseball just didn't exist to me. It was an American sport, and I was English. I knew about the NFL, because a school friend had lived in the States and came home talking about the Los Angeles Rams a lot. He was the coolest kid in school because of that. Or maybe it was because he was the first kid to own a BMX bike . . .

A lot of the preconceptions I had about American sports weren't uncommon in Great Britain. Primary among those, of course, is our spluttering apoplexy at your playing for something called the World Series when—oh my effing God!—only American teams (and no more than two Canadian ones) are in the major leagues. And coming from a nation of cricketers, why the heck do you need those big gloves? Why can't you catch a ball like a real man? And why are there so many bloody commercial breaks? (I was quite good at being pompous and angry in my younger years, clearly. I managed to happily overlook that the sport I was watching most had the names of breweries, insurance companies, and electrical goods manufacturers written in big letters on the jerseys.)

The first real memory I have of baseball is of seeing *A League of Their Own* in the cinema. Britain (and the rest of the world) is constantly awash with American culture, and that culture contains lots of references to baseball. The more American movies and television I took in, the more I became aware of baseball's lexicon, without really knowing I knew it. I knew that if you had three strikes, you were out. I knew when something unexpected happened in the office, you were thrown a curveball, or it might've come out of left field. But to deal with that curveball, you had to step up to the plate and hit one out of the park. And somewhere along the line, I'd heard the names of a few players. Babe Ruth was the fat one, Lou Gehrig was the one with a disease named after him, Joe DiMaggio had gone somewhere just as a nation was turning its lonely eyes to him, apparently, and Kramer had seen him dunking his donuts.

The first time I remember even knowing the World Series was happening was 2000. I'd just moved from London to start a new job in Berlin, Germany. I would listen to the BBC World Service in the bathroom every morning and would hear their very British reporting on what a Subway Series was and what it meant to New Yorkers. When you don't know much about a sport, it's only natural that you root for the underdog. So over the course of a week, as I took a shower or brushed my teeth, I half-heartedly hoped to hear the Mets had beaten the Yankees the previous evening (I didn't get a lot of satisfaction on those mornings in Berlin). Even British people know that the Yankees are the big evil team that must be hated.

But you can't help whom you fall in love with. And I fell in love with the evil team. I ended up being a fan of the New York Yankees. About as clichéd as it gets, huh? Foreigner gets into baseball, becomes Yankees fan. I was in New York on business in the summer of 2005. I spent my days working in a windowless office on West 49th Street and passed my evenings in my hotel room, lying on the wonderfully comfortable bed, AC cranked up to arctic, flicking through TV channels. I'd watch some news, I'd watch some Fox News for laughs, I'd inevitably find at least one rerun of a Seinfeld episode and some Latin American soccer, and I caught a couple of innings of baseball here and there. We foreigners know that baseball is popular, but it made little sense to me, and the masculine trait of not wanting to be defeated, not wanting to not understand, got the better of me. It was almost like the times that I've listened to Captain Beefheart's *Trout Mask Replica* to try to understand why people say it's so great: I must be missing something. But baseball looked like it shouldn't be confusing or difficult, and those innings

I watched on TV were enough to prompt me to discuss the possibility of going to a game with my colleagues Mark and Josh. The Yankees would be playing at home over the next few days, so it was decided that we'd go to see them, not the Mets. That accident of home scheduling is all that stood between my being a Yankees fan or a Mets fan.

So on July 27, 2005, we took the D train to the Bronx to see the Yankees play the Twins. I'd be exaggerating to say it was love at first sight, but it does kinda feel that way when I think back to that evening. Those nine innings changed my life a little bit. Now, it's not like I'd had a much-needed kidney transplant or anything. But a sport that I'd never thought about past a week's worth of morning ablutions opened up in front of me, like one of those time-lapse films of a flower blooming spliced together with a Busby Berkeley finale.

There was something about the leisurely pace, the ebb and flow, the drama inherent in a sport where the ball is in play for such a small percentage of the total time, the unique proportions of the ballpark, the shape of the field, the uniforms. The fizzing joy in my head after seeing a swiftly turned double play, the one-on-one battles at

My first baseball game. Yankees vs. Twins. July 27, 2005.

the heart of a team sport . . . it all felt *right*. In the rest of my life, I like things to be mentally tidy: I make lists, I find it difficult to multitask. With baseball, there was suddenly a sport that slotted into that part of my brain. Pitcher tries to do this. Batter tries to do that. Runners move methodically around the bases, defensive plays work like clockwork. Even the little rituals, like not stepping on the foul lines or the manager physically taking the ball from a pitcher and handing it to the reliever, felt nice in my brain. Once I sat there, with two people to answer my dumb questions—*How fast is he throwing that? How do you know when an inning is over?*—the basics became easy to understand.

Johan Santana shut out the Yankees over seven innings, and despite a three-run bottom of the eighth, the Twins were fairly comfortable 7–3 winners. Three hours and forty-two minutes, by far the longest time I'd ever spent watching a live sporting event. Like a child, I wanted a souvenir of my first live baseball game. I bought a jersey from Stan's Sports World. A Yankees road jersey with a number 2 on the back; Josh had told me that even though it wasn't a bad thing to take a liking to that evening's three-hit Robinson Cano, a Jeter jersey was a safer way to spend my money. (He was right; if I'd bought a Cano jersey that night, it would've had number 22 on the back, not his current 24, and for all intents and purposes, I'd own a Roger Clemens jersey.)

Having had my first taste of live baseball, I watched more in my hotel room. Except now the game made more sense. I started to understand where exactly the strike zone was (or where the rule book said it was). I realized that the first two foul balls count as strikes, but after that they don't. All of these little puzzles I was solving gave me a better picture of the game, but I wanted to learn more and more and more.

Watching the Yankees vs. Angels 2005 ALDS in bed in Berlin.

Back in Berlin, I found myself actually missing baseball. But the modern world had a cure for my longing: some tap-tap-tapping of my credit card number on the keyboard, and I'd paid for a subscription to have access to all of Major League Baseball's games on MLB.com, in all of its 2005, average-definition, RealPlayer glory. I would stay up late to watch Yankees games that would begin around one AM and finish as *die vögels* started singing. An American friend helped me out with any questions I had, and as October approached, I was ready for my first under-the-bedsheets-watching-the-Yankees moments. The Angels won that ALDS 3–2. It was a frustrating series to watch. But it was my first taste of the playoffs, and after just a few months, my emotional attachment wasn't strong enough to be too distraught. Other than checking out a few other games here and there for the rest of the playoffs, that was it for me and baseball for a few months. There was English Premier League and German Bundesliga soccer to be watched. During the off-season, though, I found myself paying attention to the hot stove; I bought some DVDs, tried to catch up with over a century of baseball that I'd missed.

Come 2006 and 2007, I found myself scheduling vacations to New York around Yankees home stands. Suddenly, a few times a week, I was staying up till past four o'clock in the morning watching games online, getting more and more into the game's nuances.

Living in a country where very few people care about a sport you love is a strange experience. You have to take what you can, where you can get it. The Internet's existence obviously makes long-distance fan relationships possible; twenty years ago you were relegated to reading wire stories and eventually drifting into rooting for the local team. Internet or no, it's still a little strange to be so into something and have no one to talk to in a bar about Pujols' home run, Ichiro's throw, Halladay's shutout. I bought a Yankees cap, and even though Pete Doherty's words in the Libertines song "Time for Heroes" were ringing in my head ("There are fewer more distressing sights than that / Of an Englishman in a baseball cap"), I tried to get used to what it looked like on my head. I would smile if I saw a Berliner wearing an MLB team's cap, and I would inevitably feel weird about wearing a Yankees hat when most of the baseball caps one sees overseas tend to be Yankees caps, and there really can't be that many baseball fans in Berlin. I'd find myself overthinking things: *I don't want to wear it, because I don't want people to think I'm just one of those people with a New York hat because it's a fashionable logo.* (More than that, I think, a New York Yankees hat pretty much *is* the standard of what all baseball caps have to live up to in Europe, kind of like Levi's jeans, Lacoste polo shirts, and Ray-Ban aviators. It would be interesting to ask one hundred people to draw a baseball cap and see how many would draw the Yanks' logo on there.)

My conversations with an American friend living in Berlin became less and less about music and art and more and more about baseball. And when that same friend

Opposite, top: "I'm not from New York" 2010. White New Era cap, dark blue with a hand-stitched logo.

brought me a glove back from the States, I eventually found a softball team (the Prenzlauer Berg Piranhas) to play with in the fast-pitch Berlin Mixed Softball League. I could swing the bat and pretend to be a lefty Gary Sheffield. I could stand in left field and take a step forward because I got it, I got it, I got it, and it would fall on the ground ten feet behind me. And I could throw it like, well . . . I make Johnny Damon look like Raul Mondesi. There aren't many things that are more embarrassing than realizing at the age of thirty-six that you are rubbish at throwing. Really poor. But I was enthusiastic, could hit the ball, enjoyed sliding into bases, and very much enjoyed shouting at umpires and having temper tantrums. And there were German and American baseball fans to chat to. I even got to know a proper Tampa Bay Devil Rays fan (from the days when they were still the Devil Rays and still crappy).

In 2008, I was sufficiently obsessed with baseball that I decided I wanted to see some ballparks outside of the Bronx. My trip began modestly by taking the subway to Queens to see Shea Stadium before it was demolished, then by taking trains, Greyhound buses, and flights to Philadelphia, Pittsburgh, Chicago, Milwaukee, Minneapolis, Denver, Seattle, San Francisco, L.A., and San Diego. All in all, over the last few years I've been lucky enough to see eighteen major league ballparks, but that's not the best thing. The best thing . . . well, the best thing came about because of two factors: being English and being a smoker. (Terrible, I know, but I can't help where I was born.) When smokers huddle together in the small smoking areas in public places, they tend to pass the time of day by having a little chat. This seems even more prevalent at sporting events. And when those people hear an English-

BALL CAPS SEEN IN EUROPE

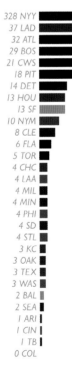

328 NYY
37 LAD
32 ATL
29 BOS
21 CWS
18 PIT
14 DET
13 HOU
13 SF
10 NYM
8 CLE
6 FLA
5 TOR
4 CHC
4 LAA
4 MIL
4 MIN
4 PHI
4 SD
4 STL
3 KC
3 OAK
3 TEX
3 WAS
2 BAL
2 SEA
1 ARI
1 CIN
1 TB
0 COL

This is hardly the height of scientific data collection, but after spending seven months in the States, I returned to Europe and started counting and making a note of all the ball caps I saw in a handful of British and German towns. The time period covered was July 2009–May 2010. Clearly, a lot of people have Yankees caps. Are they Yankees fans? Probably not. It seems to me that if you go on vacation to the city and you're looking for a souvenir to put on your head, the interlocking NY logo is a recognizable marker of the city.

Seeing less popular caps, though, made me smile a lot. When I saw a guy in a Brewers cap, I smiled. When I saw a guy in an Oakland hat, and then a few minutes later a guy in a Giants hat, I could've skipped for joy at the Bay Area–ness of it all. And seeing someone in an old-school Blue Jays cap in my hometown was wonderful. (It doesn't take much to make me happy, clearly.)

The relatively high showing of Astros caps, though, kinda tells me something: people care more about the graphic than the team. Youngsters in Germany and the UK probably like having a star on their head.

And during that whole time, I didn't see one person in a Rockies cap. Poor Colorado.

accented voice talking about baseball, nigh on all of them are interested, open, friendly, and extremely gracious. Visiting those ballparks exposed me to some truly wonderful Americans, people I never would have met had I continued singularly going to Yankees home games. That was when baseball became more than supporting my team; that was when I wanted to devour every scrap of knowledge to be devoured.

. . .

I had come to a sport in my mid-thirties and was experiencing what it was like to listen to the World Series under the covers, except that it was in my bed in Berlin and I was watching games on a laptop. I had the Internet and Photoshop instead of a handful of baseball cards and crayons. And my mind wandered and wondered: What distance is covered by base runners in a season? How big is the Green Monster compared to the Statue of Liberty? Which player has played for the most organizations? How many teams have their home dugout on the first-base side? How many Native Americans live in Cleveland? Who the hell designed that Diamondbacks logo? Baseball, being a leisurely game full of lulls and lapses, affords its fans plenty of time to ponder the game's nearly infinite significant and insignificant elements: Who was the last player called Wright to play in right field? (It was George Wright for the Expos in 1986. And, incidentally, no player called Short has ever played shortstop.) Which team's players travel the greatest distance from rookie ball to single-A, double-A, triple-A, and then the majors? Has any player ever played in all the towns Steve Miller mentions in "Rock'n Me"? What was number one on the *Billboard* Hot 100 when Nolan Ryan made his debut and then when he played his last game? Which town in the contiguous United States is the farthest from a major league team?

Baseball is endlessly fascinating to me. And probably endlessly tedious to my European friends who have to put up with me talking about why Mariano Rivera is so awesome. But they can't throw a cut fastball at 90 mph with the accuracy of a sniper, and he can. I'm still relatively new to the sport; I still feel like an interloper in your wonderful world of baseball. Every day I learn something fascinating about the universe of baseball. As I sit here typing these words on a humid summer evening in Toronto, there's a Rawlings Official Major League Baseball next to the Tic Tacs on my desk. Every time I've paused to think about a bit of sentence construction, I've picked up the ball and gripped it like in the photos I've seen on Google Images. I exhale and close my eyes, and Joe Buck informs the audience about my ERA and how I'm getting a lot more movement on my curveball this season. Tim McCarver reexplains everything Joe Buck said. It's a 3–2 count. Robinson shakes off Posada; he wants to show his best heat. He checks the runner at first, then throws it straight past Howard. The umpire signals that Howard is out! Your 2012 World Series MVP . . . Craaaaaaaig Robinson! Seriously, it's ridiculous, a man hurtling toward his forties daydreaming about winning the World Series.

I hope you enjoy the book. This is where I should finish off the introduction with something corny and basebally, like "Play ball!" right? That's not gonna happen.

Old Yankee Stadium

1860
1870
1880
1890
1900
1910
1920
1930
1940
1950
1960
1970
1980
1990
2000
2010

Formed in 1866, the Red Stockings were the first ever professional team in the 1869 and 1870 season

NABBP 1868-70

Formed in 1855; member of the NABBP from 1857-71

Founded as Union Club of Lansingburgh; NABBP member 1860-70

After dropping out of the NL, continued as an amateur team through 1878-81

Independent 1870

NABBP 1860-70

NABBP 1857-70

NABBP member in 1870 before turning pro in 1871. The team dropped out of the NAPBBP for two seasons (1872-73) following the Great Chicago Fire

In the League Alliance 1877

Both independent in 1877 and in the International Association in 1878

Cincinnati Red Stockings
Philadelphia Centennial
New Haven Elm Citys
St. Louis Red Stockings
Keokuk Western
Baltimore Marylands
Elizabeth Resolutes
Philadelphia White Stockings
Eckford of Brooklyn
Middletown Mansfields
Washington Nationals
Washington Blue Legs
Washington Nationals
Baltimore Canaries
Brooklyn Atlantics
Fort Wayne Kekiongas
Rockford Forest Citys
Troy Haymakers
Washington Olympics
Cleveland Forest Citys
St. Louis Brown Stockings
Hartford Dark Blues
Athletic of Philadelphia
Mutual of New York
Boston Red Stockings
Chicago White Stockings
Louisville Grays
Cincinnati Reds
Milwaukee Grays
Indianapolis Blues
Providence Grays
Syracuse Stars
Troy Trojans
Cleveland Blues
Buffalo Bisons
Worcester Worcesters (a.k.a. Worcester Ruby Legs)
Detroit Wolverines
New York Gothams
Philadelphia Quakers
Kansas City Cowboys
Washington Nationals
Pittsburgh Alleghenys
Allegheny
Cleveland Spiders
Brooklyn Grays
Brooklyn Atlantics
Cincinnati Red Stockings
St. Louis Brown Stockings
Baltimore Orioles

National Association of Professional Base Ball Players 1871-75

The 1872 Nationals, 1873 Blue Legs, and 1875 Nationals may have been the same franchise

Union Association 1884

The Wilmington Quicksteps played in the 1883 Inter-State Association of Professional Baseball Clubs. The following season the league changed its name to the Eastern League which the Quicksteps were winning with ease. In August 1884, they replaced the Keystones in the UA and posted an impressive 2-16 record (.111). The Milwaukee Brewers and St. Paul Saints came to the US from the Northwestern League as replacement teams for respectively the Quicksteps and the Stogies. The Kansas City Cowboys replaced Altoona Mountain City

Milwaukee Brewers
St. Paul Saints (a.k.a Apostles and White Caps)
Wilmington Quicksteps
Kansas City Cowboys
Altoona Mountain City
Keystones of Philadelphia
Pittsburgh Stogies
Chicago Browns
Baltimore Monumentals
Boston Reds
Cincinnati Outlaw Reds
Washington Nationals
St. Louis Maroons
Indianapolis Hoosiers
Brooklyn Hardfords

National League 1876-present

Boston Red Caps
Boston Beaneaters
Boston Doves
Boston Rustlers
Boston Braves
Boston Bees
Boston Braves
Milwaukee Braves
Atlanta Braves

Chicago Cubs
Chicago Colts
Chicago Orphant

New York Giants
San Francisco Giants

Philadelphia Phillies
Philadelphia Blue Jays

Houston Colt 45's
Houston Astros

Brooklyn Grooms
Brooklyn Bridegrooms
Brooklyn Superbas
Brooklyn Trolley Dodgers
Brooklyn Dodgers
Brooklyn Robins
Brooklyn Dodgers
Los Angeles Dodgers

Pittsburgh Pirates

Cincinnati Reds
Cincinnati Redlegs
Cincinnati Reds

St. Louis Cardinals
St. Louis Perfectos
St. Louis Brown Stockings

NL East and West divisions created 1969

Colorado Rockies
San Diego Padres
San Francisco Giants
Los Angeles Dodgers
Arizona Diamondbacks
Houston Astros
Cincinnati Reds
Pittsburgh Pirates
Chicago Cubs
St. Louis Cardinals
Milwaukee Brewers

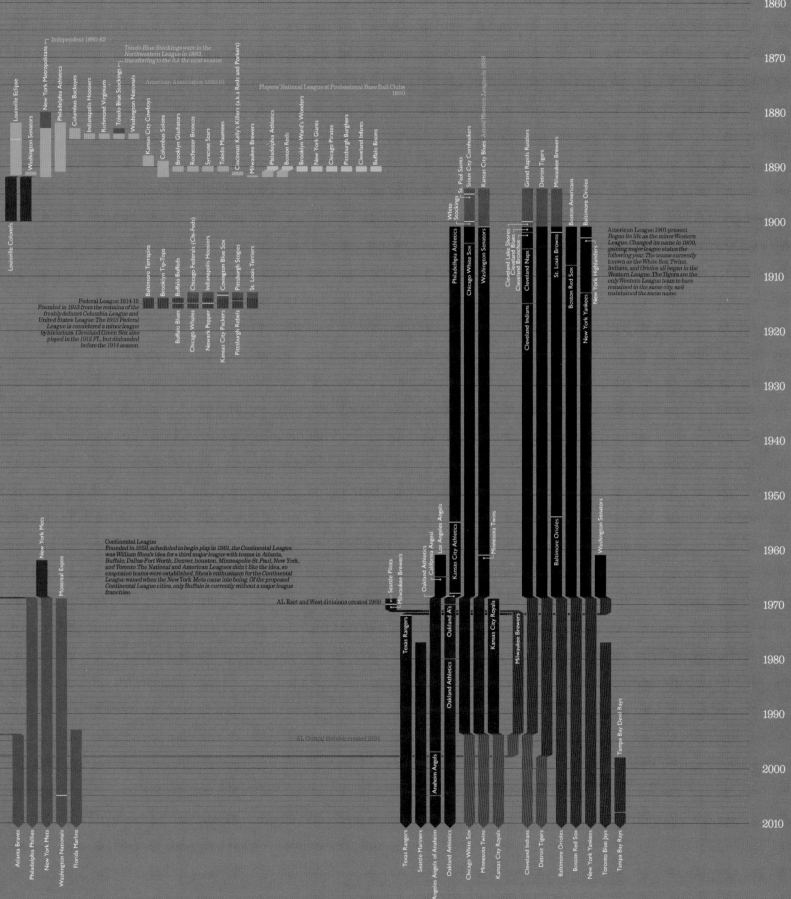

MLB RELOCATIONS

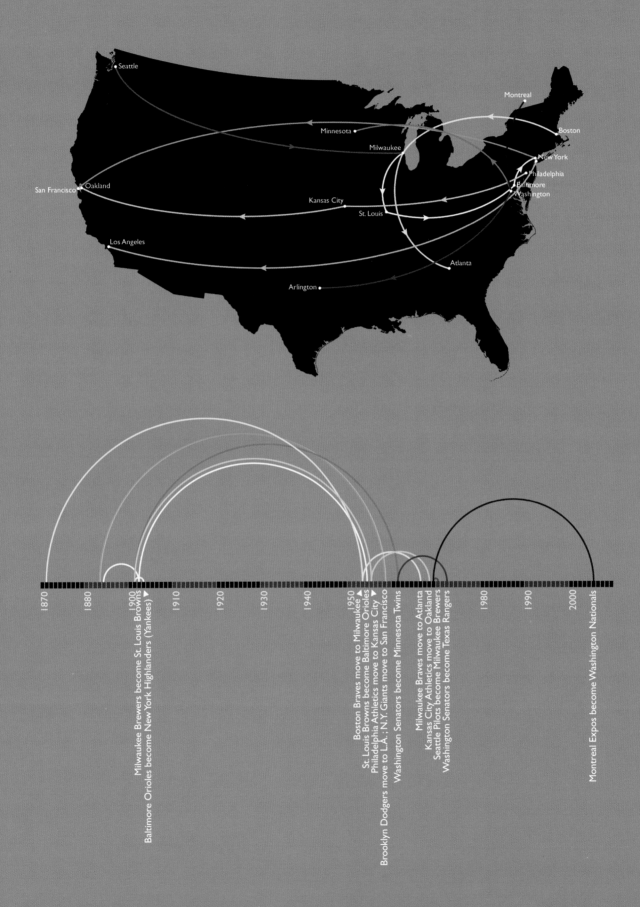

Seattle

Montreal

Boston

Minnesota

Milwaukee

New York

Philadelphia

San Francisco Oakland

Baltimore
Washington

Kansas City

St. Louis

Los Angeles

Atlanta

Arlington

1870 1880 1900 1910 1920 1930 1940 1950 1980 1990 2000

Milwaukee Brewers become St. Louis Browns

Baltimore Orioles become New York Highlanders (Yankees) ▶

Boston Braves move to Milwaukee

St. Louis Browns become Baltimore Orioles ▲

Philadelphia Athletics move to Kansas City ▶

Brooklyn Dodgers move to L.A.; N.Y. Giants move to San Francisco

Washington Senators become Minnesota Twins

Milwaukee Braves move to Atlanta

Kansas City Athletics move to Oakland

Seattle Pilots become Milwaukee Brewers

Washington Senators become Texas Rangers

Montreal Expos become Washington Nationals

EXPANSION TEAMS

FIRST FRANCHISE WIN

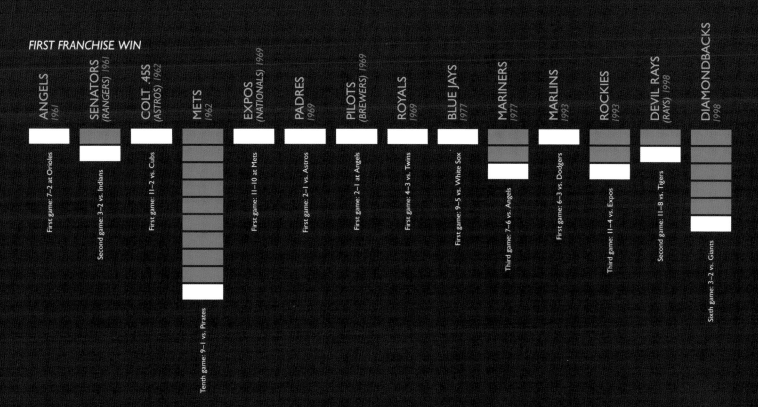

- **ANGELS** *1961* — First game: 7–2 at Orioles
- **SENATORS** (RANGERS) *1961* — Second game: 3–2 vs. Indians
- **COLT .45S** (ASTROS) *1962* — First game: 11–2 vs. Cubs
- **METS** *1962* — Tenth game: 9–1 vs. Pirates
- **EXPOS** (NATIONALS) *1969* — First game: 11–10 at Mets
- **PADRES** *1969* — First game: 2–1 vs. Astros
- **PILOTS** (BREWERS) *1969* — First game: 2–1 at Angels
- **ROYALS** *1969* — First game: 4–3 vs. Twins
- **BLUE JAYS** *1977* — First game: 9–5 vs. White Sox
- **MARINERS** *1977* — Third game: 7–6 vs. Angels
- **MARLINS** *1993* — First game: 6–3 vs. Dodgers
- **ROCKIES** *1993* — Third game: 11–4 vs. Expos
- **DEVIL RAYS** (RAYS) *1998* — Second game: 11–8 vs. Tigers
- **DIAMONDBACKS** *1998* — Sixth game: 3–2 vs. Giants

FIRST .500 SEASON, PLAYOFF APPEARANCE, PENNANT, WORLD SERIES VICTORY (UP TO AND INCLUDING 2009 SEASON)

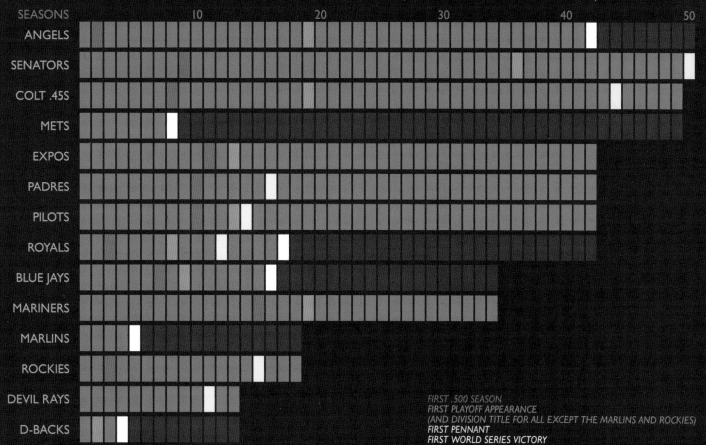

SEASONS 10 20 30 40 50

ANGELS
SENATORS
COLT .45S
METS
EXPOS
PADRES
PILOTS
ROYALS
BLUE JAYS
MARINERS
MARLINS
ROCKIES
DEVIL RAYS
D-BACKS

FIRST .500 SEASON
FIRST PLAYOFF APPEARANCE
(AND DIVISION TITLE FOR ALL EXCEPT THE MARLINS AND ROCKIES)
FIRST PENNANT
FIRST WORLD SERIES VICTORY

(IF TWO OR MORE OF THESE OCCURRED IN THE SAME SEASON
THE HIGHER OF THEM IS REPRESENTED)

TEAM NAMES
AN ETYMOLOGICAL VENN DIAGRAM

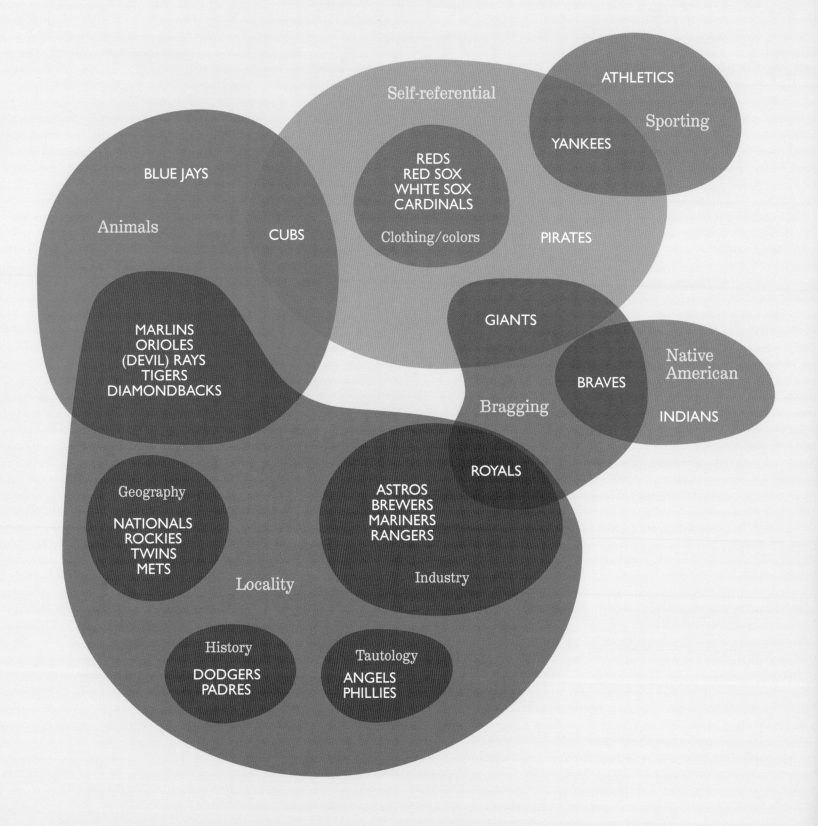

AFTER JACKIE
WHEN EACH TEAM BROKE THE COLOR LINE

1947 1948 1949 1950 1951 1952 1953 1954 1955 1956 1957 1958 1959

APRIL 15, 1947: JACKIE ROBINSON DEBUTS FOR BROOKLYN DODGERS

JULY 5, 1947: CLEVELAND INDIANS (LARRY DOBY)

JULY 17, 1947: ST. LOUIS BROWNS (HANK THOMPSON)

JULY 8, 1949: NEW YORK GIANTS (MONTE IRVIN, HANK THOMPSON)

APRIL 18, 1950: BOSTON BRAVES (SAM JETHROE)

MAY 1, 1951: CHICAGO WHITE SOX (MINNIE MINOSO)

SEPTEMBER 13, 1953: PHILADELPHIA ATHLETICS (BOB TRICE)

SEPTEMBER 17, 1953: CHICAGO CUBS (ERNIE BANKS)

APRIL 13, 1954: PITTSBURGH PIRATES (CURT ROBERTS)

APRIL 13, 1954: ST. LOUIS CARDINALS (TOM ALSTON)

APRIL 17, 1954: CINCINNATI REDS (CHUCK HARMON, NINO ESCALERA)

SEPTEMBER 6, 1954: WASHINGTON SENATORS (CARLOS PAULA)

APRIL 14, 1955: NEW YORK YANKEES (ELSTON HOWARD)

APRIL 22, 1957: PHILADELPHIA PHILLIES (JOHN KENNEDY)

JUNE 6, 1958: DETROIT TIGERS (OZZIE VIRGIL)

JULY 21, 1959: BOSTON RED SOX (PUMPSIE GREEN)

MAY 17, 1954: *BROWN VS. BOARD OF EDUCATION*

DECEMBER 1, 1955: ROSA PARKS REFUSES TO CHANGE SEATS

AUGUST 29, 1957: CIVIL RIGHTS ACT OF 1957

42

LAST PLAYERS TO WEAR THE NUMBER FOR EACH TEAM

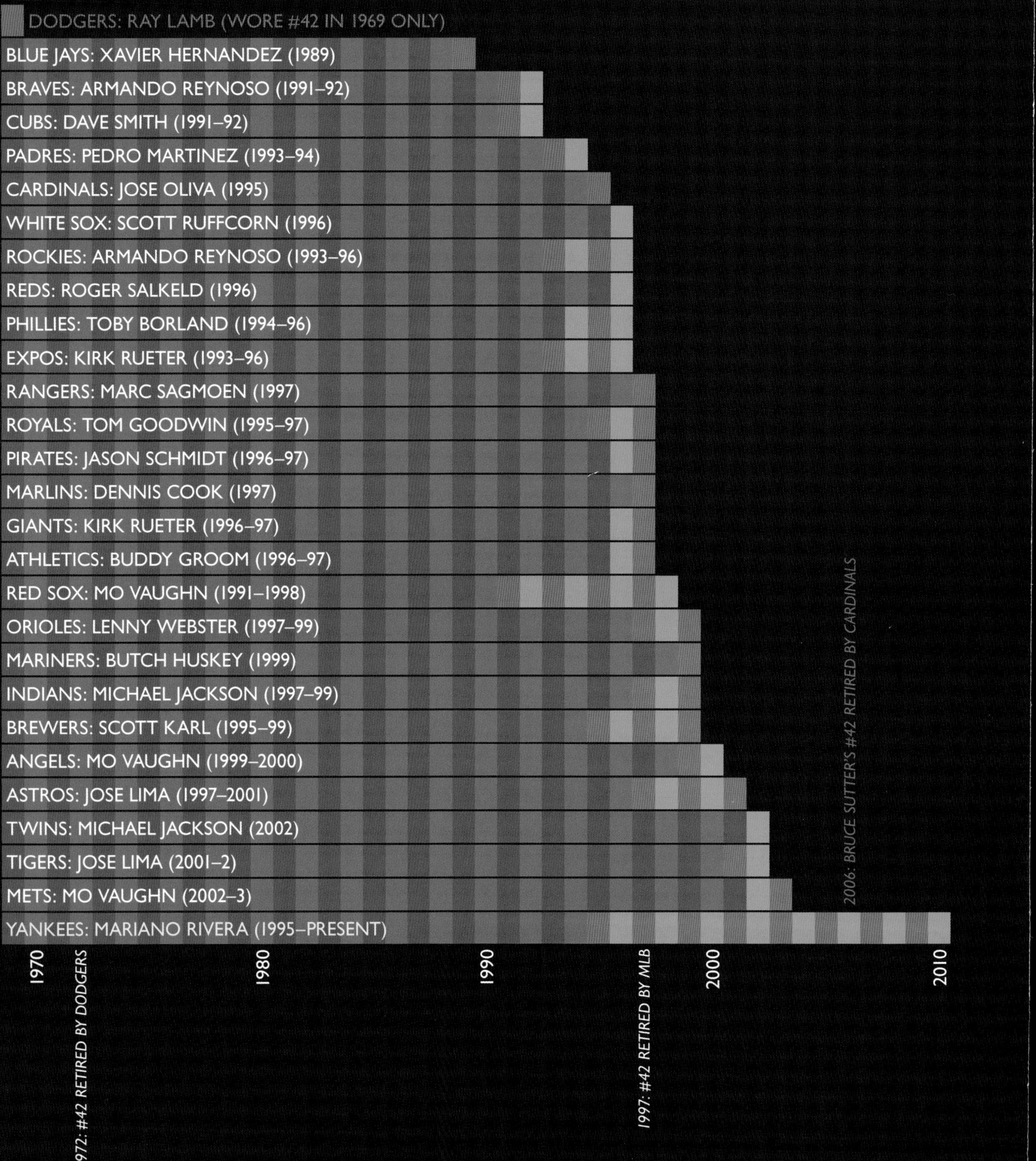

DODGERS: RAY LAMB (WORE #42 IN 1969 ONLY)

BLUE JAYS: XAVIER HERNANDEZ (1989)

BRAVES: ARMANDO REYNOSO (1991–92)

CUBS: DAVE SMITH (1991–92)

PADRES: PEDRO MARTINEZ (1993–94)

CARDINALS: JOSE OLIVA (1995)

WHITE SOX: SCOTT RUFFCORN (1996)

ROCKIES: ARMANDO REYNOSO (1993–96)

REDS: ROGER SALKELD (1996)

PHILLIES: TOBY BORLAND (1994–96)

EXPOS: KIRK RUETER (1993–96)

RANGERS: MARC SAGMOEN (1997)

ROYALS: TOM GOODWIN (1995–97)

PIRATES: JASON SCHMIDT (1996–97)

MARLINS: DENNIS COOK (1997)

GIANTS: KIRK RUETER (1996–97)

ATHLETICS: BUDDY GROOM (1996–97)

RED SOX: MO VAUGHN (1991–1998)

ORIOLES: LENNY WEBSTER (1997–99)

MARINERS: BUTCH HUSKEY (1999)

INDIANS: MICHAEL JACKSON (1997–99)

BREWERS: SCOTT KARL (1995–99)

ANGELS: MO VAUGHN (1999–2000)

ASTROS: JOSE LIMA (1997–2001)

TWINS: MICHAEL JACKSON (2002)

TIGERS: JOSE LIMA (2001–2)

METS: MO VAUGHN (2002–3)

YANKEES: MARIANO RIVERA (1995–PRESENT)

2006: BRUCE SUTTER'S #42 RETIRED BY CARDINALS

1970

1972: #42 RETIRED BY DODGERS

1980

1990

1997: #42 RETIRED BY MLB

2000

2010

RETIRED NUMBERS

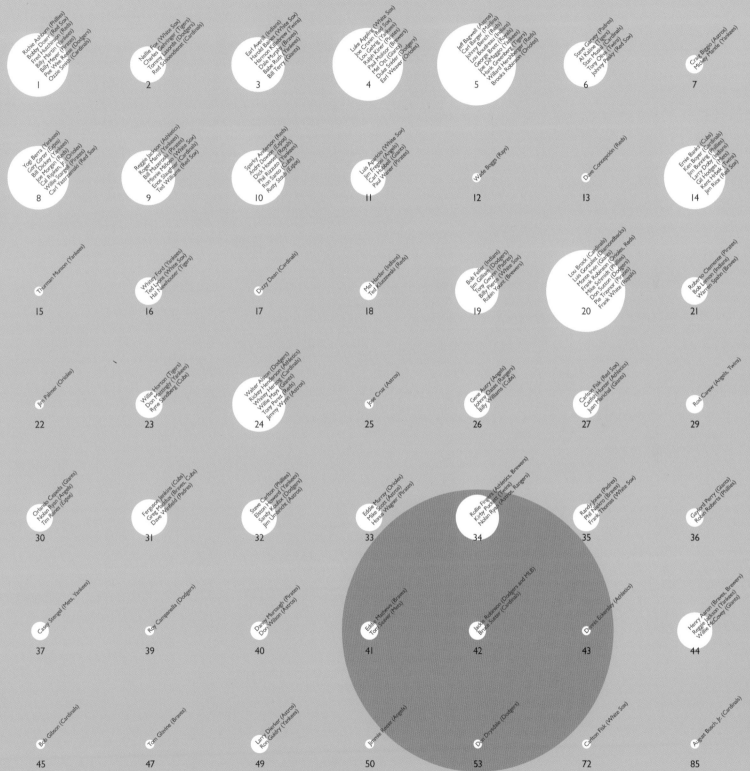

YANKEES' RETIRED NUMBERS

A PROJECTION OF WHEN THEY MIGHT RUN OUT OF DOUBLE-DIGIT NUMBERS

The Yankees, more than any other franchise, seem to love retiring numbers. So far, they've retired seventeen, including the number 8 twice. I got to wondering how long it would be before they would need to use three digits on the back of a player's uniform. The big spurt of number-retiring began with Mickey Mantle in 1969, which is where I began my projection. Not including Jackie Robinson's #42, between 1969 and 2003, the Yankees retired a number on average every 2.62 years. If they continue at that pace (which they haven't been doing up to time of going to press), and taking into account the 47 numbers needed for a 40-man roster, manager and coaches, my fairly unscientific reasoning is that the Yankees will have a player wearing the number 100 in the year 2100. Using the same methodology, the whole roster should have three-digit numbers by the year 2220.

● CAREER W/ YANKEES
◆ RETIRED NUMBER
★ ALSO HALL OF FAMER
★ RETIRED THROUGHOUT BASEBALL

★ 4 LOU GEHRIG (NUMBER RETIRED IN 1939)
★ 3 BABE RUTH (1948)
★ 5 JOE DIMAGGIO (1952)
★ 7 MICKEY MANTLE (1969)
★ 37 CASEY STENGEL (1970)
★ 8 YOGI BERRA (1972)
★ 8 BILL DICKEY (1972)
★ 16 WHITEY FORD (1974)
◆ 15 THURMAN MUNSON (1979)
◆ 9 ROGER MARIS (1984)
◆ 32 ELSTON HOWARD (1984)
★ 10 PHIL RIZZUTO (1985)
◆ 1 BILLY MARTIN (1986)
★ 44 REGGIE JACKSON (1993)
◆ 23 DON MATTINGLY (1997)
★ 42 JACKIE ROBINSON (1997)
◆ 49 RON GUIDRY (2003)

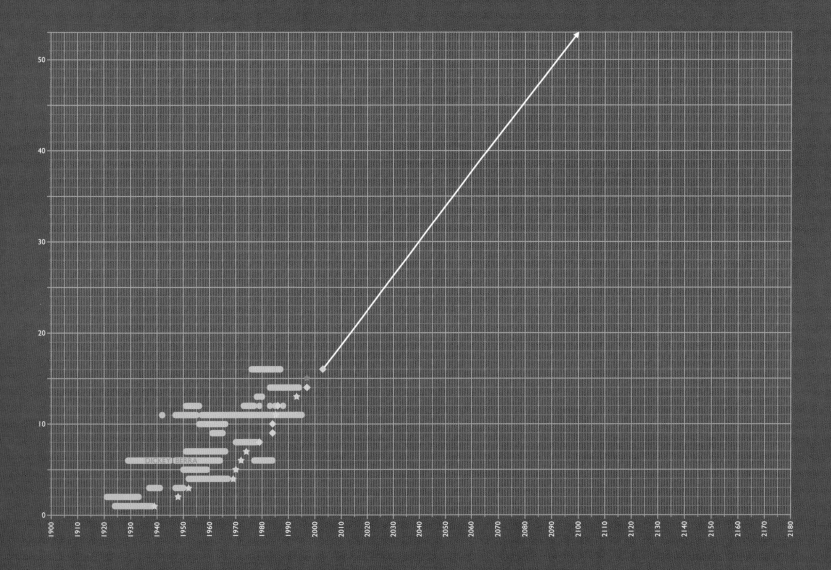

HALL OF FAME

PERCENTAGE OF MAJOR LEAGUE PLAYERS IN THE HALL OF FAME

OF THE 17,228 PLAYERS TO HAVE EVER PLAYED IN THE MAJORS (AS OF JUNE 23, 2010),
ONLY 232 OF THEM HAVE ENTERED THE HALL OF FAME (UP TO AND INCLUDING ANDRE DAWSON).
THAT'S 1.35%—ONE HALL-OF-FAMER FOR EVERY 74.26 PLAYERS.

BOBBY COX
AND ALL THE OTHER MLB MANAGERS DURING COX'S TIME WITH THE BRAVES

	1990	1991	1992	1993	1994	1995	1996	1997	1998	1999	2000

RUSS NIXON — BOBBY COX

FRANK ROBINSON — JOHNNY OATES — PHIL REGAN — RAY MILLER

JOE MORGAN — BUTCH HOBSON — JIMY WILLIAMS

DON ZIMMER — JOE ALTOBELLI — JIM ESSIAN

JEFF TORBORG — GENE LAMONT — TERRY BEVINGTON — JERRY MANUEL

LOU PINIELLA — TONY PEREZ — RAY KNIGHT

JOHN MCNAMARA — MIKE HARGROVE — CHARLIE MANUEL

DON BAYLOR

SPARKY ANDERSON — BUDDY BELL — LARRY PARRISH

RENE LACHEMANN — COOKIE ROJAS — JOHN BOLES

ART HOWE — TERRY COLLINS — LARRY DIERKER — MATT GALANTE

JOHN WATHAN — BOB SCHAEFER — BOB BOONE — TONY MUSER

HAL MCRAE — MARCEL LACHEMANN — JOE MADDON

DOUG RADER — MIKE SCIOSCIA

TOMMY LASORDA — BILL RUSSELL — GLENN HOFFMAN

TOM TREBELHORN — PHIL GARNER — DAVEY LOPES

TOM KELLY

DAVEY JOHNSON — BUD HARRELSON — MIKE CUBBAGE — DALLAS GREEN

BUCKY DENT — STUMP MERRILL — BUCK SHOWALTER

TONY LARUSSA

NICK LEYVA — JIM FREGOSI

JIM LEYLAND

JACK MCKEON — GREG RIDDOCH — JIM RIGGLEMAN — BRUCE BOCHY

ROGER CRAIG — DUSTY BAKER

JIM LEFEBVRE — BILL PLUMMER

WHITEY HERZOG — RED SCHOENDIENST — MIKE JORGENSEN

JOE TORRE — LARRY ROTHSCHILD

BOBBY VALENTINE — KEVIN KENNEDY

CITO GASTON — GENE TENACE — TOBY HARRAH — MEL QUEEN — TIM JOHNSON

BUCK RODGERS — TOM RUNNELLS — FELIPE ALOU

2001 2002 2003 2004 2005 2006 2007 2008 2009 2010

BOB BRENLY   AL PEDRIQUE   A.J. HINCH   Diamondbacks
                                                                                         KIRK GIBSON
                                                                                         Braves
                          LEE MAZZILLI   SAM PERLOZZO   DAVE TREMBLEY   JUAN SAMUEL
                                                                                         Orioles
          GRADY LITTLE   TERRY FRANCONA   Red Sox
    JOE KERRIGAN
                                                                                         Cubs
          BRUCE KIMM   MIKE QUADE
                          OZZIE GUILLEN   White Sox
                                                                                         Reds
                    DAVE MILEY
          JOEL SKINNER   Indians
          ERIC WEDGE
    CLINT HURDLE   Rockies
    LUIS PUJOLS   ALAN TRAMMELL   Tigers
                                              JOE GIRARDI   FREDI GONZALEZ   EDWIN RODRIGUEZ
                                                                                         Marlins
                                                        CECIL COOPER   DAVE CLARK   Astros
          JOHN MIZEROCK   TREY HILLMAN BRAD MILLS
          TONY PENA   Royals
                                                                                         Angels
JIM TRACY   Dodgers
          JERRY ROYSTER   NED YOST   DALE SVEUM   Brewers
          RON GARDENHIRE   Twins
                                        WILLIE RANDOLPH   Mets
                                                                                         Yankees
          KEN MACHA   BOB GEREN   Athletics
LARRY BOWA   GARY VARSHO   Phillies
LLOYD MCCLENDON   PETE MACKANIN   JOHN RUSSELL   Pirates
                                                    BUDDY BLACK   Padres
                                                                                         Giants
          BOB MELVIN   JOHN MCLAREN   DON WAKAMATSU   Mariners
                                                                                    DAREN BROWN
                                                                                         Cardinals
                                                                                         Rays
JERRY NARRON   RON WASHINGTON   Rangers
BUCK MARTINEZ   CARLOS TOSCA   JOHN GIBBONS   Blue Jays
                                              MANNY ACTA   Expos/Nationals

HOME RUNS & PEDS
WHICH OF THE TOP 25 HOME RUN HITTERS ARE TAINTED

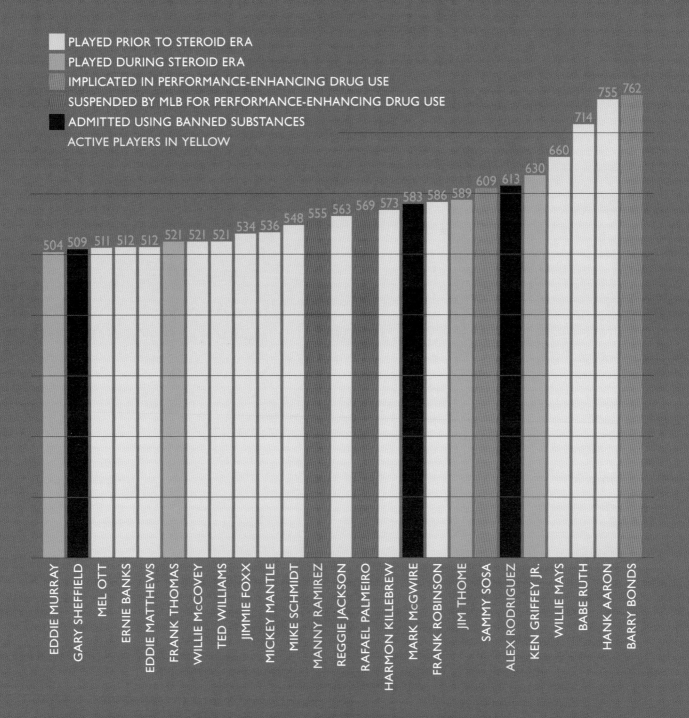

PLAYED PRIOR TO STEROID ERA
PLAYED DURING STEROID ERA
IMPLICATED IN PERFORMANCE-ENHANCING DRUG USE
SUSPENDED BY MLB FOR PERFORMANCE-ENHANCING DRUG USE
ADMITTED USING BANNED SUBSTANCES
ACTIVE PLAYERS IN YELLOW

Player	Home Runs
EDDIE MURRAY	504
GARY SHEFFIELD	509
MEL OTT	511
ERNIE BANKS	512
EDDIE MATTHEWS	512
FRANK THOMAS	521
WILLIE McCOVEY	521
TED WILLIAMS	521
JIMMIE FOXX	534
MICKEY MANTLE	536
MIKE SCHMIDT	548
MANNY RAMIREZ	555
REGGIE JACKSON	563
RAFAEL PALMEIRO	569
HARMON KILLEBREW	573
MARK McGWIRE	583
FRANK ROBINSON	586
JIM THOME	589
SAMMY SOSA	609
ALEX RODRIGUEZ	613
KEN GRIFFEY JR.	630
WILLIE MAYS	660
BABE RUTH	714
HANK AARON	755
BARRY BONDS	762

SINGLE SEASON HOME RUN RECORD
GAME-BY-GAME PROGRESSION OF RECORD FOR EACH LEADER

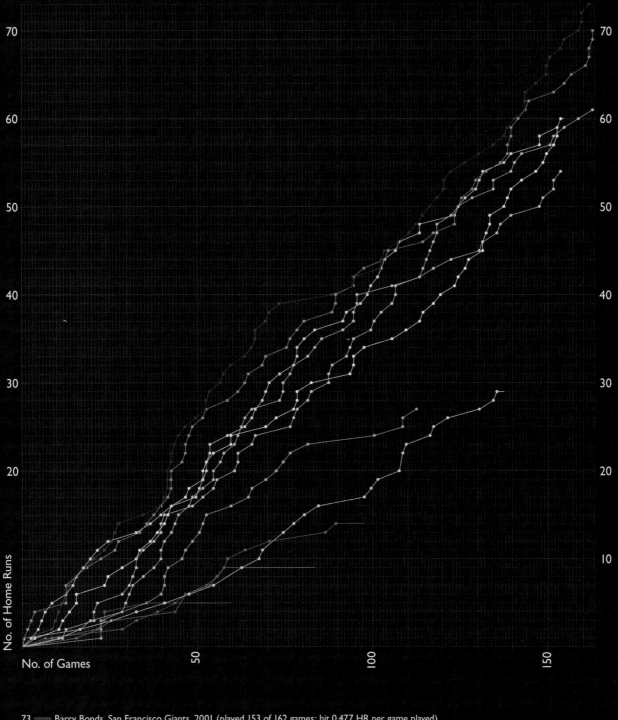

No. of Home Runs

No. of Games

73 ━━━ Barry Bonds, San Francisco Giants, 2001 (played 153 of 162 games; hit 0.477 HR per game played)
70 ━━━ Mark McGwire, St. Louis Cardinals, 1998 (played 155 of 163 games; hit 0.452 HR per game played)
61 ━━━ Roger Maris, New York Yankees, 1961 (played 161 of 163 games; hit 0.379 HR per game played)
60 ━━━ Babe Ruth, New York Yankees, 1927 (played 151 of 155 games; hit 0.397 HR per game played)
59 ━━━ Babe Ruth, New York Yankees, 1921 (played 152 of 153 games; hit 0.388 HR per game played)
54 ━━━ Babe Ruth, New York Yankees, 1920 (played 142 of 154 games; hit 0.380 HR per game played)
29 ━━━ Babe Ruth, Boston Red Sox, 1919 (played 130 of 138 games; hit 0.223 HR per game played)
27 ━━━ Ned Williamson, Chicago White Stockings, 1884 (played 107 of 113 games; hit 0.252 HR per game played)
14 ━━━ Harry Stovey, Philadelphia Athletics, 1883 (played 94 of 98 games; hit 0.149 HR per game played)
 9 ━━━ Charley Jones, Boston Red Caps, 1879 (played 83 of 84 games; hit 0.108 HR per game played)
 5 ━━━ George Hall, Philadelphia Athletics, 1876 (played 60 of 60 games; hit 0.083 HR per game played)

1998 HOME RUN CHASE
McGWIRE'S, SOSA'S, AND GRIFFEY'S HOME RUNS, DAY BY DAY

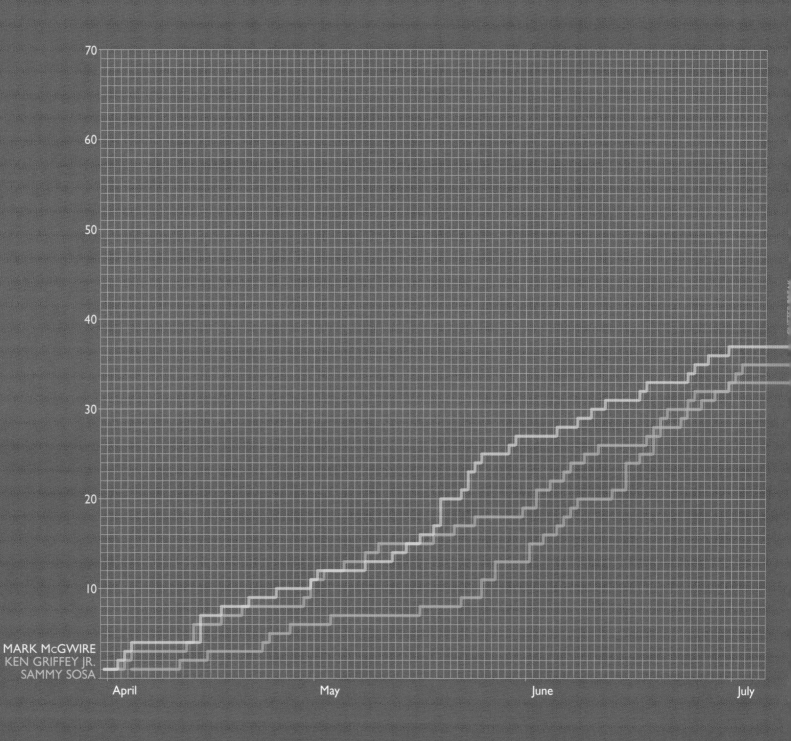

MARK McGWIRE HIT 31.4% OF THE CARDINALS' 223 HOME RUNS IN 1998

SAMMY SOSA HIT 31.1% OF THE CUBS' 212 HOME RUNS IN 1998

KEN GRIFFEY JR. HIT 23.9% OF THE MARINERS' 234 HOME RUNS IN 1998

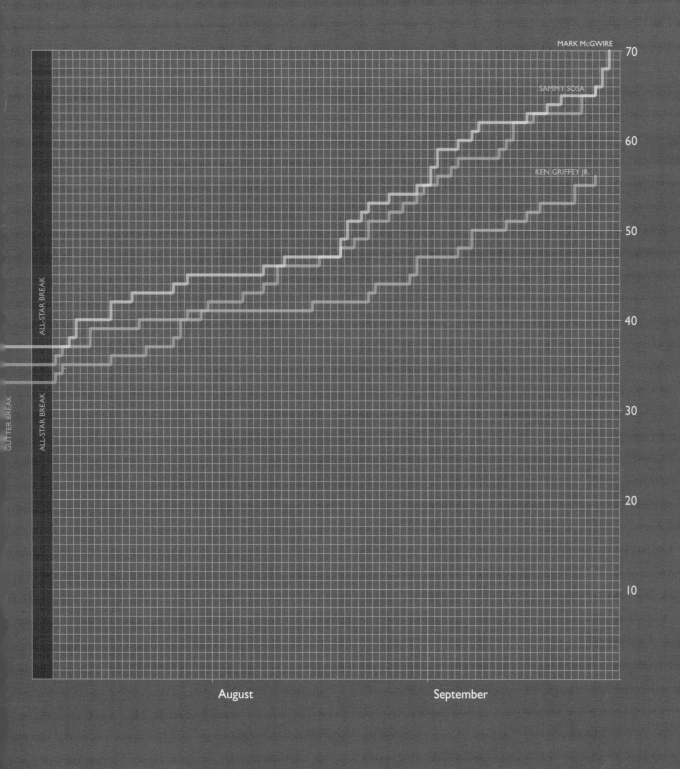

MARK McGWIRE

SAMMY SOSA

KEN GRIFFEY JR.

GUTTER BREAK

ALL-STAR BREAK

ALL-STAR BREAK

70

60

50

40

30

20

10

August

September

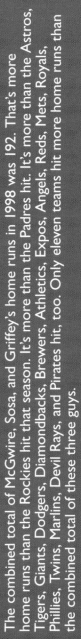
The combined total of McGwire, Sosa, and Griffey's home runs in 1998 was 192. That's more home runs than the Rockies hit that season. It's more than the Padres hit. It's more than the Astros, Tigers, Giants, Dodgers, Diamondbacks, Brewers, Athletics, Expos, Reds, Mets, Royals, Phillies, Twins, Marlins, Devil Rays, and Pirates hit, too. Only eleven teams hit more home runs than the combined total of these three guys.

BARRY BONDS' WALKS
43.6 MILES WORTH OF 'EM

AT&T PARK

BARRY BONDS CURRENTLY HOLDS
THE RECORD FOR CAREER WALKS.
DURING HIS 22 SEASONS, HE WALKED
2,558 TIMES (611 FOR THE PIRATES,
1,947 FOR THE GIANTS).

2,558 MULTIPLIED BY 90 FEET EQUALS
230,200 FEET, OR 43.6 MILES.

IF HE WALKED IN A STRAIGHT LINE
EXTENDING FROM HOME PLATE AT
AT&T PARK, OVER FIRST BASE, AND
ON AND ON FOR 43.6 MILES; THIS IS
THE ROUTE HE'D TAKE.

BONDS WOULD NEED TO BE ABLE TO
WALK ON WATER AND WALK
THROUGH WALLS TO ACHIEVE THIS. I
HAVE NO CONCRETE PROOF THAT
BONDS CAN'T DO THESE THINGS.

HE'D PROBABLY HAVE TO WALK
THROUGH A LOT OF PRIVATE
PROPERTY, TOO. BUT ONE WOULD
IMAGINE THAT WOULDN'T BE TOO
MUCH OF A PROBLEM BECAUSE HE'S
BARRY BONDS, NOT A KNOWN
BURGLAR. AND FRANKLY, IF BARRY
BONDS WALKED THROUGH A WALL
IN MY HOUSE, HIS TRESPASSING
WOULD BE THE LEAST OF MY
CONCERNS.

MAJOR LEAGUE FIELDS

Angels, Astros, Athletics, Blue Jays, Braves,
Brewers, Cardinals, Cubs, Rays, Diamondbacks,
Dodgers, Giants, Indians, Mariners, Marlins,
Mets, Nationals, Orioles, Padres, Phillies,
Pirates, Rangers, Reds, Rockies, Royals,
Red Sox, Tigers, Twins, White Sox, Yankees

MAJOR LEAGUE BALLPARKS

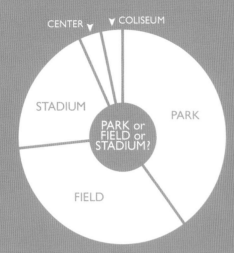

CENTER ▾ ▾ COLISEUM

STADIUM — PARK or FIELD or STADIUM? — PARK

FIELD

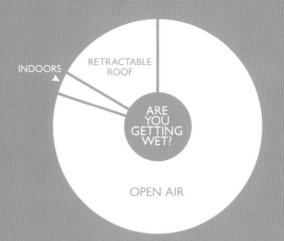

INDOORS ◂ RETRACTABLE ROOF

ARE YOU GETTING WET?

OPEN AIR

PARK: *Oriole Park (BAL), Fenway Park (BOS), Great American Ball Park (CIN), Comerica Park (DET), Minute Maid Park (HOU), Miller Park (MIL), Citizens Bank Park (PHI), PNC Park (PIT), Petco Park (SD), AT&T Park (SF), Rangers Ballpark (TEX), Nationals Park (WAS).* **FIELD:** *Chase Field (ARI), Turner Field (ATL), Wrigley Field (CHC), Progressive Field (CLE), Coors Field (COL), U.S. Cellular Field (CWS), Target Field (MIN), Citi Field (NYM), Safeco Field (SEA), Tropicana Field (TB).* **STADIUM:** *Sun Life Stadium (FLA), Kauffman Stadium (KC), Angel Stadium (LAA), Dodger Stadium (LAD), Yankee Stadium (NYY), Busch Stadium (STL).* **CENTER:** *Rogers Centre (TOR).* **COLISEUM:** *Oakland Coliseum (OAK).*

OPEN AIR: *Turner Field (ATL), Oriole Park (BAL), Fenway Park (BOS), Wrigley Field (CHC), Great American Ball Park (CIN), Progressive Field (CLE), Coors Field (COL), U.S. Cellular Field (CWS), Comerica Park (DET), Sun Life Stadium (FLA), Kauffman Stadium (KC), Angel Stadium (LAA), Dodger Stadium (LAD), Target Field (MIN), Citi Field (NYM), Yankee Stadium (NYY), Oakland Coliseum (OAK), Citizens Bank Park (PHI), PNC Park (PIT), Petco Park (SD), AT&T Park (SF), Busch Stadium (STL), Rangers Ballpark (TEX), Nationals Park (WAS).* **INDOORS:** *Tropicana Field (TB).* **RETRACTABLE ROOF:** *Chase Field (ARI), Minute Maid Park (HOU), Miller Park (MIL), Safeco Field (SEA), Rogers Centre (TOR).*

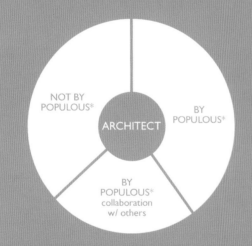

NOT BY POPULOUS* — ARCHITECT — BY POPULOUS*

BY POPULOUS* collaboration w/ others

DIRTY — PURE

NAMING RIGHTS?

OWNER

BY POPULOUS: *Oriole Park (BAL), Progressive Field (CLE), Coors Field (COL), U.S. Cellular Field (CWS), Comerica Park (DET), Sun Life Stadium (FLA), Minute Maid Park (HOU), Target Field (MIN), Citi Field (NYM), Yankee Stadium (NYY), AT&T Park (SF), Busch Stadium (STL).* **POPULOUS COLLABORATION:** *Great American Ball Park (CIN; w/ GBBN Architects), Angel Stadium (LAA; renovations w/ Walt Disney Imagineering), Citizens Bank Park (PHI; Ewing Cole Cherry Brott), PNC Park (PIT; w/ L.D. Astorino & Associates), Petco Park (SD; w/ Antoine Predock; Spurlock Poirier; ROMA), Tropicana Field (TB; w/ Lescher & Mahoney Sports; Criswell, Blizzard & Blouin Architects), Nationals Park (WAS; w/ Devrouax & Purnell).* **OTHER:** *Chase Field (ARI; Ellerbe Becket), Turner Field (ATL; Heery International; Rosser International; Williams-Russell and Johnson; Ellerbe Becket), Fenway Park (BOS; Osborne Engineering Corp.), Wrigley Field (CHC; Zachary Taylor Davis), Kauffman Stadium (KC; Kivett and Myers), Dodger Stadium (LAD; Captain Emil Praeger), Miller Park (MIL; HKS, Inc.; NBBJ; Eppstein Uhen Architects), Oakland Coliseum (OAK; Skidmore, Owings and Merrill; HTNB), Safeco Field (SEA; NBBJ; 360 Architecture), Rangers Ballpark (TEX; David M. Schwarz/Architectural Services, Inc.; HKS, Inc.), Rogers Centre (TOR; Rod Robbie).*

* Until March 2009, Populous was known as HOK Sport.

PURE: *Oriole Park (BAL), Fenway Park (BOS), Kauffman Stadium (KC), Angel Stadium (LAA), Dodger Stadium (LAD), Yankee Stadium (NYY), Oakland Coliseum* (OAK), Rangers Ballpark (TEX), Nationals Park (WAS).* **DIRTY:** *Chase Field (ARI), Great American Ball Park (CIN), Progressive Field (CLE), Coors Field (COL), U.S. Cellular Field (CWS), Comerica Park (DET), Sun Life Stadium (FLA), Minute Maid Park (HOU), Miller Park (MIL), Target Field (MIN), Citi Field (NYM), Citizens Bank Park (PHI), PNC Park (PIT), Petco Park (SD), Safeco Field (SEA), AT&T Park (SF), Busch Stadium (STL), Tropicana Field (TB).* **OWNER:** *Turner Field (ATL; named after former owner Ted Turner), Wrigley Field (CHC; after former owner William Wrigley Jr.), Rogers Centre (TOR; named after Rogers Communications, the building's current owners).*

* Offered a renewal of naming contract to McAfee. They declined.

GREEN MONSTER
HEIGHT COMPARISONS

The Green Monster at Fenway Park (37 ft 2 in), Marine Corps War Memorial (78 ft), the O from the Hollywood sign (45 ft), Ted Williams (6 ft 3 in), Robert Wadlow (world's tallest man, 8 ft 11 in), NFL regulation goalposts (40 ft), Statue of Liberty (151 ft)

DIAMONDS IN MANHATTAN
EVERY PLACE TO PLAY BASEBALL OR SOFTBALL IN MANHATTAN

At the Polo Grounds on September 18, 1963, Ted Schreiber of the New York Mets grounded into a double play to end a 5-1 defeat by the Phillies. That was the last professional baseball game to be played in Manhattan. There are, though, still plenty of places—in parks, school yards, and on artificial turf—where children and adults alike can use a bat and ball and live out their fantasies of being Derek Jeter or Jose Reyes.

PARKING LOTS AT MLB STADIUMS
SOME OF THEM ARE AESTHETICALLY PLEASING FROM ABOVE

ANGEL STADIUM OF ANAHEIM
ANAHEIM, CA

KAUFFMAN STADIUM NOT OF ANAHEIM
KANSAS CITY, MO

DODGER STADIUM ALSO NOT OF ANAHEIM
LOS ANGELES, CA

MILLER PARK NOT OF GODDAMN ANAHEIM
MILWAUKEE, WI

ROADS INCLUDED IF THEY GO ONLY TO THE PARKING LOT.
MOST OTHER BALLPARKS HAVE BORING PARKING LOTS.

ROAD TRIP

By 2008, my baseball habit was getting serious. Watching games on the Internet and going to a couple of Yankees games a season wasn't enough. Coming to baseball later in life meant that there were endless amounts of culture and history, all of this being there, that I hadn't experienced. I needed a crash course beyond *Yankeeographys* and a Ken Burns box set—intermediate fieldwork in seeing baseball outside of the Bronx. I put together a loose plan, checking team schedules with the vague route that I wanted to take: east to west across the top, then down the West Coast.

My first stop, though, was only a few miles away: Shea Stadium for a Mets-Dodgers game. Santana vs. Kuroda. Aside from being the first non-Yankees game I'd been to, it was the first time I'd been to a game where I had no rooting interest, and the first time I'd seen pitchers hitting. Shea, of course, had a reputation that preceded it. I'd only ever heard bad things about Shea as a ballpark. But more than that, for most of my life (and I'd imagine for most British people in general), the name Shea Stadium is connected with the Beatles' concert in 1965: beautiful color images of Ed Sullivan introducing them, John, Paul,

View from the highest seat in right field at Shea Stadium.

George, and Ringo running onto the field with their instruments from the dugout onto a stage behind second base, all of those New York policemen dashing around trying to stop people from running toward the stage.

Honestly, Shea wasn't as bad as I'd expected. My mate Derick and I chatted the evening away over a few beers and hot dogs, one of the game's aces in front of us. As the game progressed, we wandered round, sitting in different sections, and inadvertently began doing something that I've since tried to do at as many ballparks as possible: sitting in the farthest seat from the plate, the top corner seat in the upper deck. Baseball seems so far away from that seat, it only enhances the oddity of the game's shapes.

Then I was off to Penn Station to catch the Amtrak, and my road trip (track trip?) felt like it was properly beginning. Once the train emerges from the tunnel in New Jersey, things start to look less like New York and more like America. I loved that journey; sixteen-year-old Craig, the Craig who loved *On the Road*, would have been super-proud of his mid-thirties self. But mid-thirties Craig was justifiably proud of himself for getting out of the vacuum of MLB.TV and Yankee Stadium. I arrived at 30th Street Station in Philadelphia, bought a subway token, checked the map, asked a nearby guy if I was on the right platform. I was, and we got to chatting when we got onto the train. Brendan was going to the Phillies-Reds game, too. He offered me a tallboy. There I was: about to see a new ballpark, in a city I'd just arrived in, drinking beer out of a brown paper bag with a friendly stranger. We chatted away, and I explained for the first of what later would feel like hundreds of times about how an Englishman got into baseball. At the game, the woman seated next to me tried to convince me that I should support the Phillies and not the Yankees, but she wasn't going to give me a hard time about it 'cause her dad was a Yankees fan. Ken Griffey Jr.

was stuck on 599 home runs, much to the amusement of a Phillies fan behind me ("Griffey! You're a bum!"). A long fly ball to center field was the closest he came that day. Cole Hamels threw a shutout for the Phils.

After the game, I got my first taste of a Greyhound station. For about four hours, waiting to get a bus to Pittsburgh, I was given a crash course in *la vie Greyhound. Do you have a spare cigarette? Do you have any change? Do you have a couple of bucks so that I can get back home to see my sick mother?* And, oddly, *Anyone wanna buy a brick?* He meant it, too: stood there with a slightly disturbing look in his eyes, holding the brick over his head like a meth-addicted version of the Statue of Liberty. The sixish-hour journey started to make the sheer size of the States more real for me. Back in England, there aren't many journeys that take six hours; here I'd not even left Pennsylvania. I arrived shortly after dawn, and it was already hot. The cabdriver took me to a hotel in the shadow of PNC Park. Michael Jackson's "Rock with You" came on the radio in the cab. We chatted about Michael and how great he was back then; the cabbie turned to me and told me that if he had Michael's money, he could "guaran-*tee* that I'd have a great effing time." At the ticket office across the street from the hotel, a man who looked like Dick Cheney seemed delighted as I told him about my road trip. His voice got a wee bit sadder when he started talking about how his father had long promised to take him on a similar tour but had never gotten around to it before he died.

PNC Park was stunning. But you don't need me to tell you that. I got a Richie Hebner bobblehead. (You really wouldn't believe how many times during my trip I got Richie out of my backpack and bobbled his head.) PNC is a no-smoking facility. But, after moving around to the upper deck, above the third-base line, I noticed a guy having a sneaky one right at the top. I walked up there to

The heads, shoulders, and thighs of Wrigley Field.

join him, and I had my first War on Terror conversation. The guy seemed to be suspicious of me right away. He had a glass eye, which, when combined with his suspicious nature, made him almost a caricature. After a brief chat about smoking and the game, he turned to me and asked, "Do you hate America?" I assured him that I didn't. I knew I was in for a conversation where I'd have to bite my tongue about my pinko political views. The highlight of what he had to say in his They-Started-It rant was telling me that he "didn't give an eff" if Muslims built a mosque next door to his house as long as they didn't "fly any more effing planes into our buildings." And that if there really were seventy-two virgins waiting in heaven for him, he'd (pointing to the Roberto Clemente Bridge) "jump off that effing bridge right now!"

The next morning, back at the Greyhound station, I was befriended by a guy in a Red Sox cap, a guy who was the sort of person who would probably beat the crap out of me if he'd met me in another situation. He was a truck driver who laughed at his own unfunny jokes and had wild eyes that made me a bit nervous. He sat behind me; thankfully, there was a nicer person to chat with

in front of me. Mike was an eighteen-year-old soldier on his way home from Fort Bragg, North Carolina, to Missoula, Montana, for a twelve-day break. He seemed at once older than his age (the army training, I assume) and exactly his age when he talked about girls, beer, and stuff he liked to do (get with girls and drink beer). I was glad to have him as a smoking companion at every stop we pulled up to. Every now and again, something of importance would come into his head to distract him from his Star Wars novel and the shooting game on his

Me, smoking at **U.S. Cellular Field,** looking down upon the smoking section.

cell phone, and he'd turn around and tell me something about being a soldier. It usually involved being drunk or shooting. He offered me three magazines to read. *Guns & Ammo* was one of them; the others were called *Practical Shooter* and *Technical Shooter.* When I politely declined the offer, he spent the next twenty minutes explaining all about different bullets and what damage they could do. I wished I'd just taken the magazines. He owned a .30-06 but wanted the weapon on the cover of one of the magazines, a thing that looked like it could kill an elephant on the other side of a brick wall. Mike and I had one last smoke together when we arrived in Chicago. I wished him luck and hoped that his army career would be a safe one; he wished me luck in the States and told me to be careful, 'cause there are some crazy people out there.

When I was telling people about my road trip, Wrigley Field was the one park everyone immediately asked about. Much like the association in my head between Shea and the Beatles, Wrigley is *The Blues Brothers* and Ferris Bueller for me. The day game I went to (and it *had* to be a day game) was a wee bit special, too: a throwback game in celebration of the sixtieth anniversary of Chicago Cubs baseball on WGN-TV. Ushers wore straw boaters, the Cubs wore their old unis, and the Braves wore Boston Braves unis. And I got to see my first-ever and, to date, only bases-loaded walk-off hit-by-pitch in the eleventh inning.

After Wrigley, my expectations for U.S. Cellular Field couldn't have been much lower. As I left my hotel for the park, I reflected that I was visiting the South Side park only because it happened to be in the same city as Wrigley. But in a lot of ways, seeing the White Sox's home was a far more enjoyable experience. Since I had no expectations for it to live up to, the utter friendliness of everyone I came into contact with there was all the

Larry Yount's brother.

more appreciated, from the woman on the subway who patiently explained why Sox fans were better than Cubs fans and insisted on showing me the old Comiskey Park home plate plaque in the parking lot to the fellow smokers whom I joined in surreptitiously having a crafty one on the open-air exit ramps ('cause the smoking area was all the way downstairs) and the beer vendor who overlooked the rules and served a thirty-seven-year-old Englishman who didn't have any valid ID with him. Perhaps some of the friendliness may have been down to the new cap I'd bought outside Wrigley, a Montreal Expos cap. After a few games in different stadiums, having to accept that my Yankees cap would elicit several shouts of "Yankees suck," I got a wee bit bored, and because of the beauty of the old three-color Expos cap and their rest-in-peace-ness as a team, I didn't feel like I was *really* cheating on the Yankees. The effect was immediate. At every subsequent game, the Expos cap brought a positive reaction.

From Chicago I headed up to Milwaukee to see baseball under a roof. Well, at least the pregame preparations were under a roof. But sunny weather led to the roof being opened for the game. Joined by my pal

The Hubert H. Humps-My-Humps-My-Lovely-Lady-Lumphreydome.

Rebecca, I boarded a bus to the stadium. Sure enough, the Expos cap got me talking to a frumpy middle-aged woman. She asked where in the UK I was from, and I told her I was from Lincoln. She noted that the city has a rather splendid cathedral. (It does. Google it.) We chatted all the way to Miller Park, mostly consisting of her reciting a canned history of the Brewers. At the game, I missed the sausage race 'cause I went for a leak. Miller Park's best feature? Having an actual bar in the ballpark. A bar where you can drink beer, smoke cigarettes, and pretend that you're not at the game, but instead far away at a bar watching the game.

At the Greyhound station in Milwaukee to get an overnight bus to the Twin Cities, I took an empty seat next to a hipster-looking guy. Sometimes it can be difficult to tell whether someone's the bass player in an ironically named band and really into Terry Richardson or a work-release parolee with deep-seated racist tendencies. This guy was the latter. Joy. He started telling me how he hates his country, how he's never been outside of the States, and how he probably wouldn't be allowed because he's

been in prison. Further joy. Also he added that people in Milwaukee don't like him because he's white. Okaaay . . . A few sentences later, it became clear that a main source of his problems might have had something to do with the fact that he was an enormous racist. At around the same point, I noticed that there were two white people in the whole station. One of them was an English tourist in an Expos cap, and the other was telling the tourist that he didn't like the, ahem, "coloreds."

I let Ku Klux Hipster get on the bus before me so I could choose a seat as far away from him as possible. The bus cut through the night like, well, er, like a rather loud, slow bus. We passed the Alliant Energy Center in Madison, Wisconsin, which was advertising two forthcoming shows, the incongruity of which made me chuckle to myself: Poison in concert and a talk by His Holiness the fourteenth Dalai Lama. I was still smiling to myself as we passed a gas station that claimed to be "a great place to take a leak." America wasn't all racist maniacs.

It had to happen sooner or later: going to a ballpark that was horrible. The Hubert H. Humphrey Metrodome, aside from Rod Carew doing some pregame stuff on the field, had very little to praise. And for whatever reason, I didn't get to experience any of the famed Minnesota Nice. The friendliest people I spoke to were foreign: Canadians at the game and a Kenyan cabdriver. Oh, one good thing that the Hubert H. Humps-My-Humps-My-Lovely-Lady-Lumphreydome did have was revolving doors, because of the need to keep the air pressure up inside the building, and to stop the roof flopping down upon Joe Mauer's head. After the game, though, when I left, people were just going out of the emergency doors, which are your bog-standard (non-revolving) doors. At that point, there's a really fun rush of air, like you've suddenly stepped into a cartoon hurricane. So, y'know, go Twins!

After Minnesota it was time for a not particularly frugal but oh so worthwhile detour to Denver and Coors Field. In the shuttle bus from the airport, a businessman from Detroit tried to convert me into a Tigers fan. A woman who looked like a drunk Liza Minnelli in a Dustin Diamond wig was listening in on our conversation and proudly boasted that her neighbor's son was (and is) journeyman catcher Gregg Zaun.

The cabdriver from the hotel to lower downtown Denver was a friendly old fella. His grandfather had moved from southwest England to work in the mines in Colorado because it paid better than the mines in Cornwall. Up before dawn, twelve hours down the mine, home after dusk, six and a half days a week. And there I was flouncing around, going to watch a baseball game.

Coors Field is beautiful. Its beauty isn't hindered by what you can see beyond the ballpark: the Rocky Mountains. At dusk, it's even more impressive, the mountains purple under purple, peach, and orange clouds. I'm waiting for the day that Oscar Niemeyer designs a

The most gorgeous view in baseball.

ballpark for an expansion team in Rio de Janeiro. Until then, Coors Field has the best view. It's not just the view, though; it's a park where you can walk all the way around and not miss a moment of the game. There were $4 bleacher tickets, and with a bit of help from my fake posh English accent, I got myself into a better section by playing the tourist-taking-photos card. I'd noticed ushers and stadium employees were friendly in some places and strict in others. Denver, Seattle, Pittsburgh, and San Diego were all nice-usher parks. Another lovely thing about Coors Field is the landscaped area in center field, next to the visitors' bullpen, with trees, a rock garden, a small waterfall, and fountains, and a grass path from the bullpen all the way around. I stood over the bullpen and watched catcher Yamid Haad of the visiting Indians slowly walk along the path, checking out the landscaping. The melancholy sight of a catcher wandering 'round, lost in thought, was made only more melancholy when I later found out Haad was designated for assignment that very day, without having played a single game for the Indians

Yamid Haad at Coors Field.

Ichiro.

(or, for that matter, anyone in the majors since 2005).

The next stop was Seattle. I'd made it from New York to the Pacific Northwest in a leisurely three weeks. I arrived while the Mariners were on a road trip, so after a few days lounging around with my friends Lisa and Cameron in Wenatchee, Washington, taking advantage of the lovely weather and the refreshingly cold water of Lake Chelan, I went to see my first game where a significant number of fans of the visiting team were in attendance. It was the night before Canada Day, and the Blue Jays

were in town. And there were a lot of Canadians in town. Suddenly my Expos cap was, well, normal. Roy Halladay threw a complete-game shutout, so nothing extraordinary happened that night.

A couple of long car journeys took me as far as Eureka, California, via a few days at the Oregon Country Fair with my friends Kraig and Barbara, and then another long bus journey landed me in San Francisco. The bus broke down in Cloverdale, so we all had to get off and spend an hour milling around, chatting. It was a really nice

Underneath the bench in the home team dugout at Oakland-Alameda County Coliseum.

hour, too. No one got angry, and I had a nice natter with a guy who was returning to the Bay Area after relocating to Eureka to live with his girlfriend of three years. Two weeks after the move, she dumped him.

I arrived in the Bay Area while the All-Star break was going on, so the only thing I could do in Oakland was take the stadium tour. And I was a bit worried whether I could actually get on the tour. The A's website clearly states "no walk-ups" for stadium tours. Undeterred, I made plans to walk up. I hopped on the BART train, a fantastic-looking subway system with chunky, angular trains that look like airbrushed sci-fi depictions of a better world.

The "no walk-ups" thing was easily gotten around, seeing as though there was only one other person taking the tour. And it was a fun tour. I've only been on one other stadium tour (old Yankee Stadium), a way more polished experience, I suppose, 'cause it was the Yankees. Donnie, our Coliseum tour guide, began by giving us a calendar with pictures of A's players cuddling up to puppies, and took us around the restaurant area, the expensive corporate boxes, and then the guts of the stadium. We got to see the indoor batting cage that the teams use, and he gave us each a baseball. My first real-life proper baseball. All scuffed up, like it really had been used. We went into the visitors' clubhouse. It's kinda what you'd expect in there: it looks like the closets of thirty motel rooms all crammed into one low-ceilinged room. The selection of DVDs was by far the most interesting sight: *Wedding Crashers, Old School, S.W.A.T., Happy Gilmore, Eddie Murphy: Delirious, The Transporter, Ocean's Eleven, Jackass: The Movie, 61*, Rocky, Rocky II, Rocky III, Rocky IV, Rocky V* . . .

The clubhouse kitchen looked like any office kitchen. Except this one, rather than tea, coffee, and sandwiches with names scrawled on them with a Sharpie, had a crapload of bottled water, Gatorade, bubble gum, candy,

Giants fan listening to some Styx.

ice cream, and sunflower seeds. Donnie offered us ice creams. Mmmm, Choco Taco. And then he took us to sit in the home team's dugout. There was loads of bubble gum stuck underneath the bench. And at the end of the dugout: a toilet cubicle. Oh. My. God! Reggie Jackson, Catfish Hunter, Dennis Eckersley, Rickey Henderson, and, er, Jason Giambi probably all took a dump right there!

Across the bay at AT&T Park, I saw Tim Lincecum pitch in his first game after missing his All-Star Game start because of illness. He lost this game. But there were magnificent garlic fries, so things evened out. (An aside: That game's closer was Brian Wilson. A friend of mine in Berlin, young guy, around twenty-two, Giants fan, was looking through my CDs and saw all of my Beach Boys stuff, including some Brian Wilson solo records. He pulled out Wilson's debut solo album and chuckled, saying, "This guy's got the same name as the Giants closer!" Made me feel old.)

After arriving at LAX and dropping off my stuff in a cheap hotel in Hollywood, I went straight to Union Station to get the train out to Anaheim, specifically Angel Stadium of Anaheim, to watch the Los Angeles Angels of Anaheim play the Cleveland Indians of, er, Cleveland. Watching Angels games on TV, I'd always kinda hated the phony mountainside stuff with the geysers and fireworks, especially when you compare the current stadium to the older incarnation with its big, beautiful Googie "A" scoreboard. I'm one of those fuddy-duddies who hates fireworks after home team home runs, so I secretly enjoyed it when Indians center fielder Grady Sizemore hit the game's first home run. The chorus of groans and boos was lovely to hear, which made up for the ostentatious, showy *shoom-bang* of fireworks when the Angels' Jeff Mathis hit one out of the park a few innings later. But as

The Angels win.

in most of the other stadiums I've been to, the people I talked to were all nice. An old fella came along when I was smoking in the designated area and we shared a chat about how the modern world is making us all soft. There was a couple seated next to me who had a tiny baby, and all the people around us, who seemed to also be season ticket holders, greeted the couple and their new addition passionately. It was neat to see the community among the denizens of the section.

I had to leave the game with an inning to go so I could catch the last train back to L.A. at the ungodly hour of a quarter past ten. I stood on the platform with the floodlit stadium looming across the parking lot, listening to the roars of the crowd as the last three Indians hitters tried and failed to mount a comeback.

I hopped in a taxi at Union Station and spent the next fifteen minutes with Tim, the chattiest cabdriver I've ever known. Almost immediately he shook my hand and introduced himself. And he spent way too much of the journey looking at me and not nearly enough of it looking at, you know, the road.

Dodger Stadium was the winner: my favorite ballpark, and the most wonderful-looking sports venue I've ever seen. Even describing its location is fantastic. Dodger Stadium is a great name; Dodger Stadium sits in Chávez Ravine. And its address is 1000 Elysian Park Avenue, after the Elysian Fields, the final resting place of the souls of the heroic and virtuous. I arrived an hour or so before the gates opened, not to be sure I got a Brad Penny bobblehead but rather to take a nice slow walk around the parking lots. Dodger Stadium looks fantastic when it's empty, gray tarmac all around, broken up by UFO-like planters holding beautifully sculpted trees. The stadium itself is a delight, the colors and shapes a perfect example of the time. It's a ballpark that fits perfectly with its city

Sanford.

and immediate environment. The game itself almost didn't matter; on this one-off visit, the ballpark was always going to be the star. The Dodgers beat the Nats 3–2, though. Game over, Randy Newman's "I Love L.A."—one of my favorite songs—escorted me out of the stadium, back to my hotel room to sleep, and to Union Station the next morning to board the train to San Diego.

Petco Park was the last stadium, the fifteenth on a two-month trip from coast to coast. After ballparks named after an antivirus software company, a bank, an insurance company, a financial services corporation, a chewing gum baron, two breweries, and two telecommunications companies, a ballpark named after a pet store. And I was there to see the Padres play the Diamondbacks, the team with my least favorite uniforms, a team I'd already seen three times on my trip. Because San Diego was the last stop on my trip, I splurged on a ten-rows-behind-the-home-dugout seat. But even having sat in the champagne seats, I think the nicest part of Petco Park is the Park at the Park area behind center field. When

Seriously, it doesn't get more beautiful than this.

there's not a game on, the Park at the Park is just a regular neighborhood park. On game days it must be a lovely place to watch a game. But I went and watched up close as Greg Maddux got the win and Trevor Hoffman the save. Pretty much the perfect end to my trip. And it was dollar dog night.

You'll have noticed this essay isn't entirely about baseball. But traveling across the country, seeing a whole load of ballparks, and meeting people on trains, planes, or buses all made baseball more real. Getting brief glimpses of life as a fan of the Padres or Mariners or Twins or Brewers or Pirates made me feel like more of a baseball fan. The road trip furthered my metamorphosis into a baseball fan, not just a Yankees fan. Simple things, really tiny moments, were important: a brief chat about last night's game, or simply sitting in a bar and muttering "Nice curveball" to myself at the exact time that the guy next to me said the exact same words. I'll certainly never feel like an American, and I'll always feel like a foreigner at baseball games. But baseball will never feel foreign.

Maddux wins, Hoffman gets the save. The perfect end to a road trip.

NIGHT GAMES
FIRST HOME NIGHT GAME FOR EACH OF THE PRE-EXPANSION TEAMS

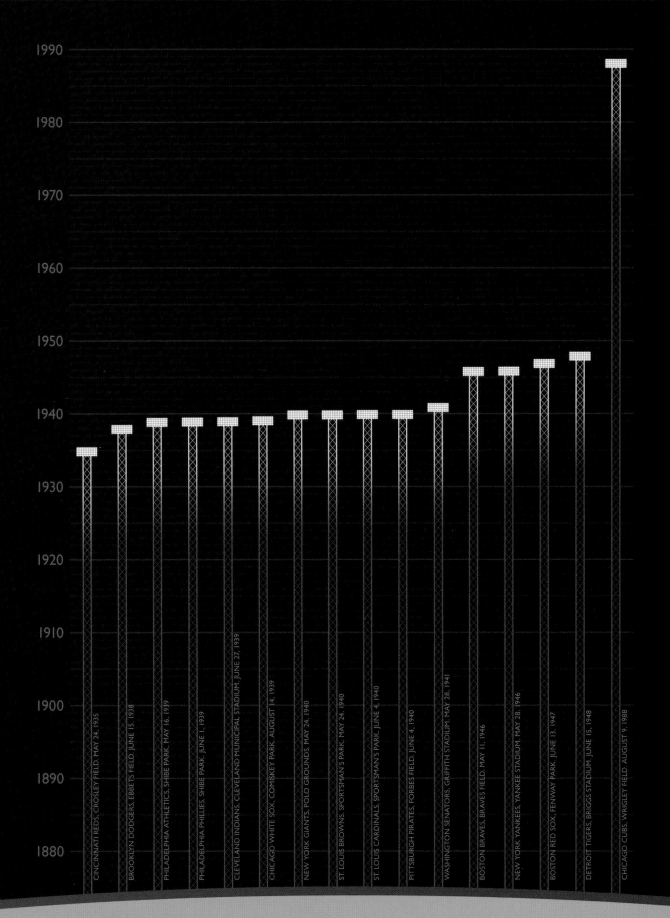

1990
1980
1970
1960
1950
1940
1930
1920
1910
1900
1890
1880

CINCINNATI REDS, CROSLEY FIELD, MAY 24, 1935
BROOKLYN DODGERS, EBBETS FIELD, JUNE 15, 1938
PHILADELPHIA ATHLETICS, SHIBE PARK, MAY 16, 1939
PHILADELPHIA PHILLIES, SHIBE PARK, JUNE 1, 1939
CLEVELAND INDIANS, CLEVELAND MUNICIPAL STADIUM, JUNE 27, 1939
CHICAGO WHITE SOX, COMISKEY PARK, AUGUST 14, 1939
NEW YORK GIANTS, POLO GROUNDS, MAY 24, 1940
ST. LOUIS BROWNS, SPORTSMAN'S PARK, MAY 24, 1940
ST. LOUIS CARDINALS, SPORTSMAN'S PARK, JUNE 4, 1940
PITTSBURGH PIRATES, FORBES FIELD, JUNE 4, 1940
WASHINGTON SENATORS, GRIFFITH STADIUM, MAY 28, 1941
BOSTON BRAVES, BRAVES FIELD, MAY 11, 1946
NEW YORK YANKEES, YANKEE STADIUM, MAY 28, 1946
BOSTON RED SOX, FENWAY PARK, JUNE 13, 1947
DETROIT TIGERS, BRIGGS STADIUM, JUNE 15, 1948
CHICAGO CUBS, WRIGLEY FIELD, AUGUST 9, 1988

THE NEAREST FIELD
EACH MLB BALLPARK'S NEAREST BASEBALL DIAMOND

Randy Johnson Baseball Field, Eastlake Park
5,275 ft from Chase Field
Phoenix, AZ

New Schools at Carver
5,557 ft from Turner Field
Atlanta, GA

Carroll Park
5,081 ft from Oriole Park at Camden Yards
Baltimore, MD

Briggs Field at M.I.T.
4,190 ft from Fenway Park
Boston, MA

Lincoln Park
3,576 ft from Wrigley Field
Chicago, IL

Armour Square Park
1,058 ft from U.S. Cellular Field
Chicago, IL

(Behind Bellevue Vets Bar, Bellevue, KY)
6,190 ft from Great American Ball Park
Cincinnati, OH

Cuyahoga Community College Metropolitan Campus
5,172 ft from Progressive Field
Cleveland, OH

Auraria Campus
4,659 ft from Coors Field
Denver, CO

Wayne State University Baseball Stadium
9,818 ft from Comerica Park
Detroit, MI

Norland Middle School
5,362 ft from Sun Life Stadium
Miami Gardens, FL

Davis High School
9,610 ft from Minute Maid Park
Houston, TX

Zimmerman Park
10,893 ft from Kauffman Stadium
Kansas City, MO

Portola Middle School
5,069 ft from Angel Stadium of Anaheim
Anaheim, CA

Elysian Park
4,194 ft from Dodger Stadium
Los Angeles, CA

Merrill Park
4,133 ft from Miller Park
Milwaukee, WI

Parade Athletic Fields
5,143 ft from Target Field
Minneapolis, MN

Leavitts Park
5,940 ft from Citi Field
New York, NY

Col. Charles Young Playground
3,216 ft from Yankee Stadium
New York, NY

Greenman Field Baseball Complex
3,560 ft from Oakland-Alameda County Coliseum
Oakland, CA

(On the corner of 7th St. and Packer Ave.)
2,214 ft from Citizens Bank Park
Philadelphia, PA

Spring Hill Playground
9,148 ft from PNC Park
Pittsburgh, PA

San Diego High School
5,853 ft from Petco Park
San Diego, CA

George R. Moscone Recreation Center
15,447 ft from AT&T Park
San Francisco, CA

Judkins Park
7,549 ft from Safeco Field
Seattle, WA

Gene Slay's Boys' Club of St. Louis
8,901 ft from Busch Stadium
St. Louis, MO

Campbell Park
1,352 ft from Tropicana Field
St. Petersburg, FL

Lamar High School
13,184 ft from Rangers Ballpark in Arlington
Arlington, TX

Riverdale Park
12,510 ft from Rogers Centre
Toronto, ON

Randall Recreation Center
3,107 ft from Nationals Park
Washington, DC

Distances are measured from home plate to home plate. An effort was made to be as accurate as possible, but in cases where the major league ballpark has a roof, the distance is approximate.

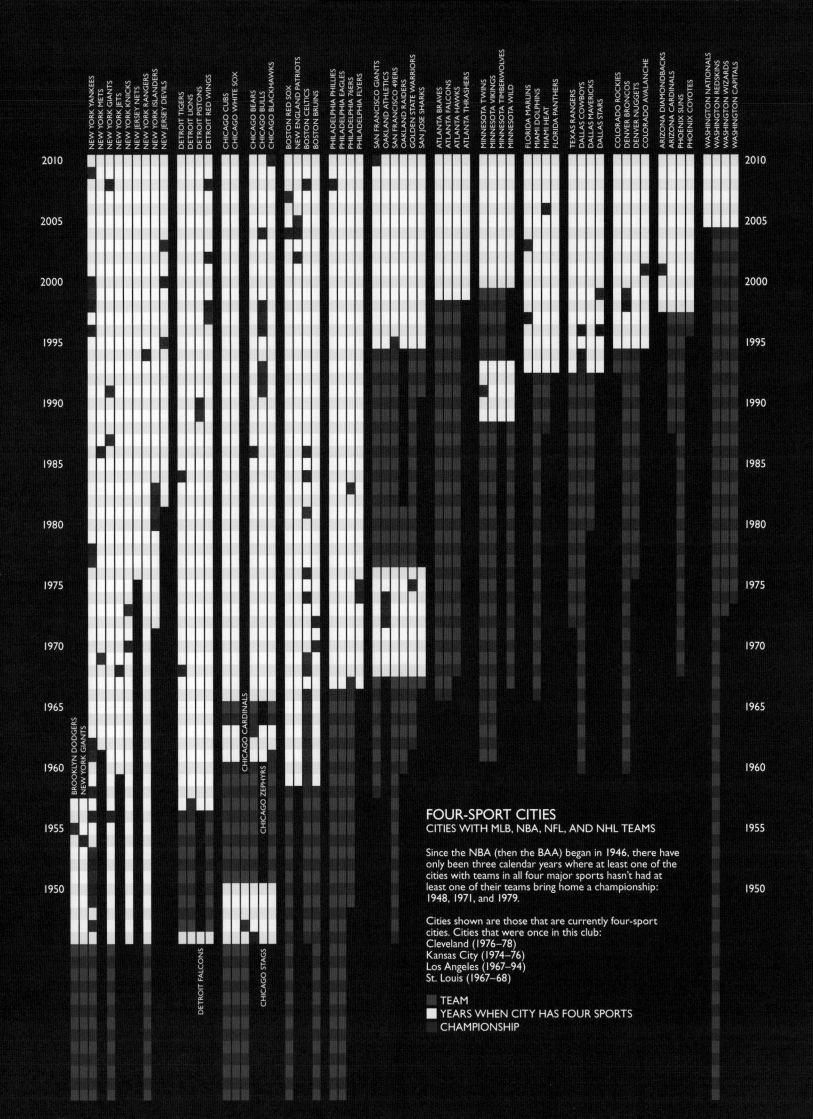

FOUR-SPORT CITIES
CITIES WITH MLB, NBA, NFL, AND NHL TEAMS

Since the NBA (then the BAA) began in 1946, there have only been three calendar years where at least one of the cities with teams in all four major sports hasn't had at least one of their teams bring home a championship: 1948, 1971, and 1979.

Cities shown are those that are currently four-sport cities. Cities that were once in this club:
Cleveland (1976–78)
Kansas City (1974–76)
Los Angeles (1967–94)
St. Louis (1967–68)

TEAM
YEARS WHEN CITY HAS FOUR SPORTS
CHAMPIONSHIP

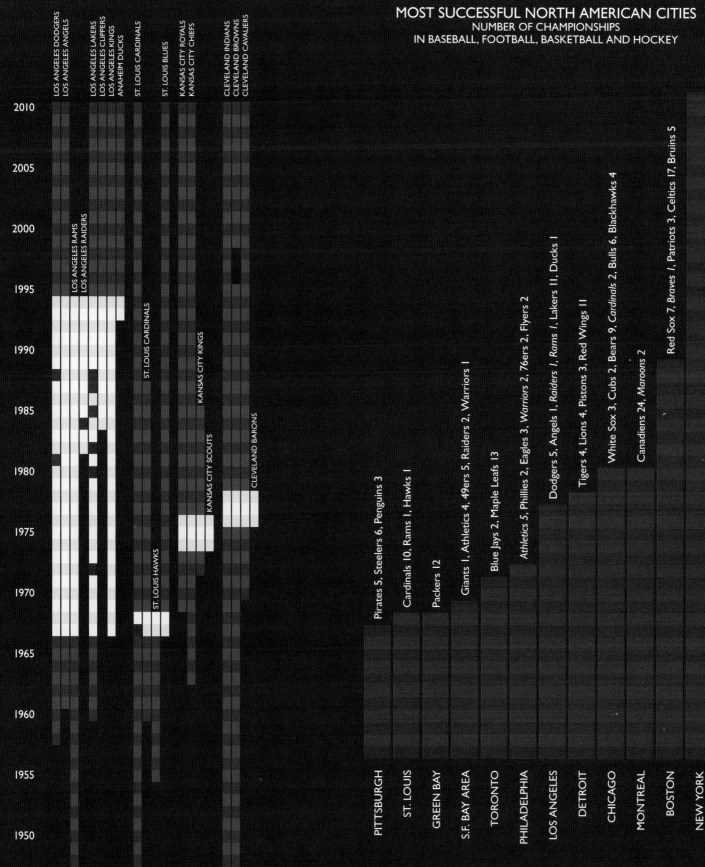

MOST SUCCESSFUL NORTH AMERICAN CITIES
NUMBER OF CHAMPIONSHIPS
IN BASEBALL, FOOTBALL, BASKETBALL AND HOCKEY

LOS ANGELES DODGERS
LOS ANGELES ANGELS
LOS ANGELES LAKERS
LOS ANGELES CLIPPERS
LOS ANGELES KINGS
ANAHEIM DUCKS
ST. LOUIS CARDINALS
ST. LOUIS BLUES
KANSAS CITY ROYALS
KANSAS CITY CHIEFS
CLEVELAND INDIANS
CLEVELAND BROWNS
CLEVELAND CAVALIERS

LOS ANGELES RAMS
LOS ANGELES RAIDERS

ST. LOUIS CARDINALS

KANSAS CITY KINGS

ST. LOUIS HAWKS

KANSAS CITY SCOUTS

CLEVELAND BARONS

2010
2005
2000
1995
1990
1985
1980
1975
1970
1965
1960
1955
1950

PITTSBURGH — Pirates 5, Steelers 6, Penguins 3

ST. LOUIS — Cardinals 10, Rams 1, Hawks 1

GREEN BAY — Packers 12

S.F. BAY AREA — Giants 1, Athletics 4, 49ers 5, Raiders 2, Warriors 1

TORONTO — Blue Jays 2, Maple Leafs 13

PHILADELPHIA — Athletics 5, Phillies 2, Eagles 3, Warriors 2, 76ers 2, Flyers 2

LOS ANGELES — Dodgers 5, Angels 1, Raiders 1, Rams 1, Lakers 11, Ducks 1

DETROIT — Tigers 4, Lions 4, Pistons 3, Red Wings 11

CHICAGO — White Sox 3, Cubs 2, Bears 9, Cardinals 2, Bulls 6, Blackhawks 4

MONTREAL — Canadiens 24, Maroons 2

BOSTON — Red Sox 7, Braves 1, Patriots 3, Celtics 17, Bruins 5

NEW YORK — Yankees 27, Giants 5, Dodgers 1, Mets 2, Giants 7, Jets 1, Knicks 2, Islanders 4, Rangers 4, Devils 3

Some of you might be thinking that it's not right to combine New Jersey's teams in New York's totals, but the way I look at it, New York's football teams play in NJ anyway, so it'd be silly not to. And you wouldn't believe the amount of emails I had on the topic of San Francisco and Oakland being separate or being combined as the Bay Area when an earlier version of this appeared on the website. Well, it was only about ten emails so it's not so unbelievable, really. Anyway, I decided to combine them. And I assume you have noticed, but in the above chart, teams that are no longer in the city listed appear in italics.

Infinite Ballfield

INFINITE BALLFIELD

One of the things I love about ballparks, aside from the eccentricities that make each one unique, is being able to see the city beyond the outfield. Sports such as soccer, football, and rugby—games played on varying sizes of rectangles—are mostly enclosed, sealed off from the world. We sit in the stands and look down at the same green rectangle. The only thing we can see outside of the stadium is the sky. If you look upward at most modern soccer stadiums, it's like a really good corporate lobby or airport terminal. Green-rectangle sports architecture can enter into the realm of the truly beautiful, especially during a night game as the sky changes color, with the grass slowly being illuminated more and more by the floodlights. It's a self-contained spectacle, and it's not that different from watching it on TV.

But (most) baseball stadiums are different. Life is going on over there. Beyond the outfield wall, the bleachers, the scoreboard, the enormous advertisements for soft drinks and automobiles—beyond all of that, people are going about their day. In Anaheim, commuters driving on the freeway; Pittsburgh, people walking across the Roberto Clemente Bridge or working late in the downtown offices; the Bronx, commuters on the 4 train; Denver, whole neighborhoods doing their thing, and—if you have exceptional eyesight—a mountain goat here or there in the Rocky Mountains.

The sense of place is especially wonderful at a day game. While *they* are working, *you* snuck off to a ballgame. As you slurp down sixteen ounces of Coca-Cola, drop peanut shells on the floor, and take off your cap for the anthem, your team takes to the field, and you relax in the sun for two or three hours. *They* are filling out spreadsheets, *you* are filling in a scorecard; the wonderful leisurely pace of the game is only heightened because you are stealing time (okay, you took a personal day, but it's more fun to convince yourself that you are stealing time from the boss).

You allow your mind to wander. Justin Morneau clobbers one. You know it's going out from the sound off the bat. It's over the wall, it's over the bleachers, the ball hawks, the concessions . . . it could just keep on going. The outfield wall is the boundary, and once it passes that boundary, it's a home run and the ball is dead, at least according to the rules. But who remembers the exact point in the air where the ball became a home run? It's where it lands that matters.

In the spectator's mind, foul lines extend outward forever. Morneau's bomb could still be flying. It's climbing over downtown Minneapolis, it's reaching cruising altitude over Lake Calhoun, over Edina, over Waseca. It's not until it crosses the state line into Iowa that the ball even starts its descent. Farmers and agribusiness executives watch as a baseball falls out of nowhere; kids playing hide-and-seek stop and look up. As fast as lightning, a Japanese man wearing a gray uniform with the word "Seattle" across the chest makes a diving catch. Emerging from a dust cloud of dry topsoil, he stands up and fires the ball back toward Minnesota. It's a bullet of a throw: Ichiro nails the runner trying to get back to second.

2009 MLB TICKET PRICES

HIGHEST & LOWEST PRICE FOR INDIVIDUAL (ADULT) GAME TICKETS

▼ MEDIAN LOWEST PRICE TICKET: $9   ▼ MEDIAN HIGHEST PRICE TICKET: $205

Team	Range
ASTROS	RANGE: $7–50
PHILLIES	$16–60
ATHLETICS	$9–55
PADRES	$9–57
WHITE SOX	$9.50–67
MARINERS	$7–65
TIGERS	$5–77
BREWERS	$8–80
ORIOLES	$8–80
BRAVES	$6–80
INDIANS	$8–85
ROCKIES	$4–100
TWINS	$8–112
GIANTS	$10–135
ANGELS	$12–200
PIRATES	$9–210
BLUE JAYS	$5–210
RANGERS	$6–220
REDS	$7–235
DIAMONDBACKS	$5–240
CARDINALS	$16–255
ROYALS	$9–250
RAYS	$10–270
METS	$11–280
RED SOX	$12–325
MARLINS	$9–325
NATIONALS	$5–335
CUBS	$9–35
DODGERS	
YANKEES	

ONE OF THE SUPER-EXPENSIVE SO-CLOSE-YOU'RE-SNIFFING-THE-UMPIRE'S-ASS-CRACK TICKETS AT YANKEE STADIUM COSTS $1,250.

THAT'S 1,250 U.S. DOLLARS, NOT ZIMBABWEAN DOLLARS.

ALTERNATIVELY, $1,250 COULD BUY YOU 312.5 TICKETS IN MLB'S CHEAPEST SEATS, THE $4 SEATS IN THE BLEACHERS AT COORS FIELD.

2009 ATTENDANCE
HIGHS, LOWS, AND AVERAGES

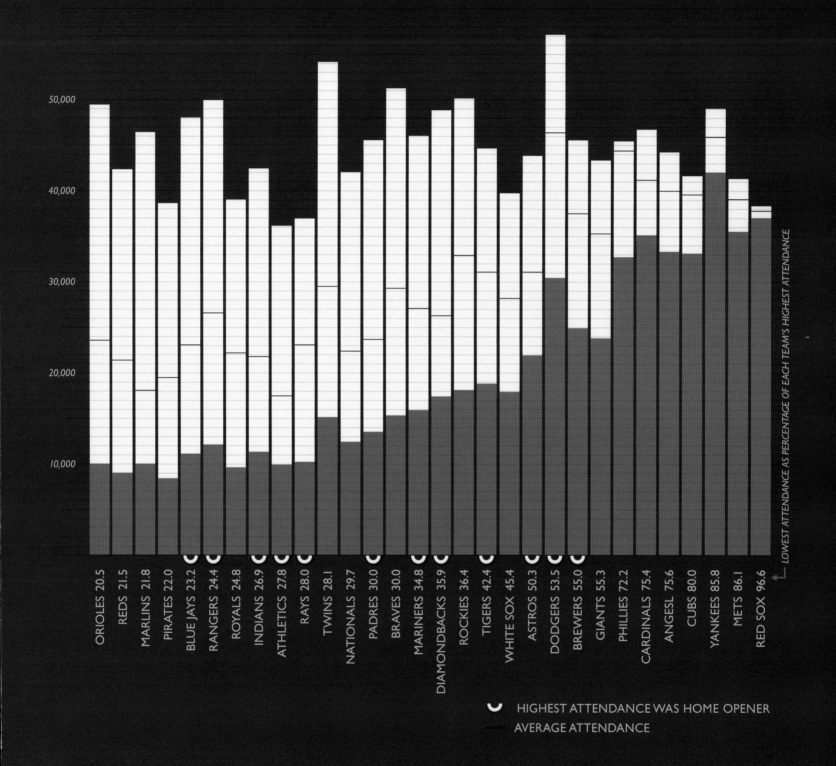

ORIOLES 20.5
REDS 21.5
MARLINS 21.8
PIRATES 22.0
BLUE JAYS 23.2
RANGERS 24.4
ROYALS 24.8
INDIANS 26.9
ATHLETICS 27.8
RAYS 28.0
TWINS 28.1
NATIONALS 29.7
PADRES 30.0
BRAVES 30.0
MARINERS 34.8
DIAMONDBACKS 35.9
ROCKIES 36.4
TIGERS 42.4
WHITE SOX 45.4
ASTROS 50.3
DODGERS 53.5
BREWERS 55.0
GIANTS 55.3
PHILLIES 72.2
CARDINALS 75.4
ANGELS 75.6
CUBS 80.0
YANKEES 85.8
METS 86.1
RED SOX 96.6

LOWEST ATTENDANCE AS PERCENTAGE OF EACH TEAM'S HIGHEST ATTENDANCE

HIGHEST ATTENDANCE WAS HOME OPENER
AVERAGE ATTENDANCE

$9–650

HOME TEAM DUGOUTS
FIRST- OR THIRD-BASE LINE?

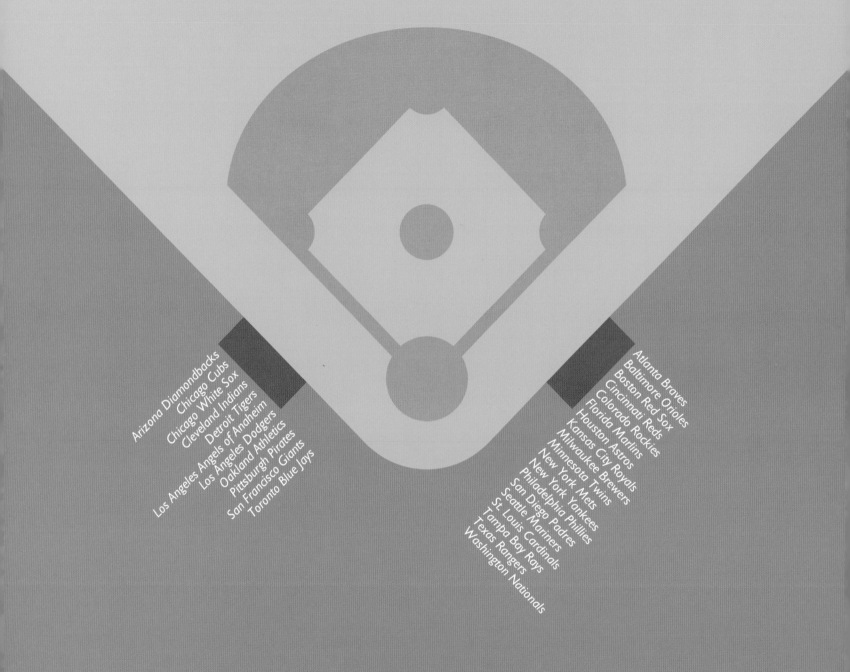

Arizona Diamondbacks
Chicago Cubs
Chicago White Sox
Cleveland Indians
Detroit Tigers
Los Angeles Angels of Anaheim
Los Angeles Dodgers
Oakland Athletics
Pittsburgh Pirates
San Francisco Giants
Toronto Blue Jays

Atlanta Braves
Baltimore Orioles
Boston Red Sox
Cincinnati Reds
Colorado Rockies
Florida Marlins
Houston Astros
Kansas City Royals
Milwaukee Brewers
Minnesota Twins
New York Mets
New York Yankees
Philadelphia Phillies
San Diego Padres
Seattle Mariners
St. Louis Cardinals
Tampa Bay Rays
Texas Rangers
Washington Nationals

BALLPARK ORIENTATION
DIRECTION THE BATTER IS FACING IN ALL MLB PARKS

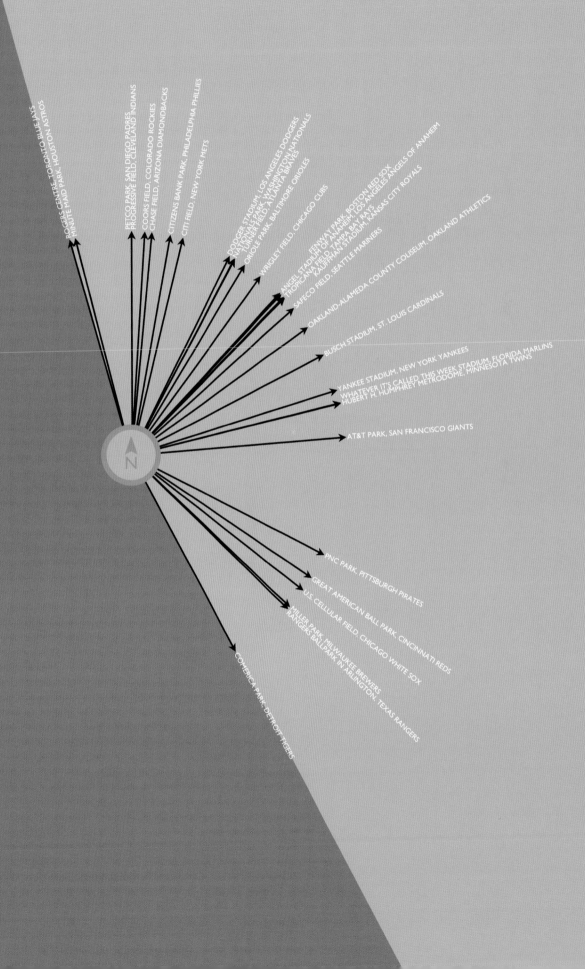

ROGERS CENTRE, TORONTO BLUE JAYS
MINUTE MAID PARK, HOUSTON ASTROS

PETCO PARK, SAN DIEGO PADRES
PROGRESSIVE FIELD, CLEVELAND INDIANS
COORS FIELD, COLORADO ROCKIES
CHASE FIELD, ARIZONA DIAMONDBACKS
CITIZENS BANK PARK, PHILADELPHIA PHILLIES
CITI FIELD, NEW YORK METS

DODGER STADIUM, LOS ANGELES DODGERS
NATIONALS PARK, WASHINGTON NATIONALS
TURNER FIELD, ATLANTA BRAVES
ORIOLE PARK, BALTIMORE ORIOLES

WRIGLEY FIELD, CHICAGO CUBS

FENWAY PARK, BOSTON RED SOX
ANGEL STADIUM OF ANAHEIM, LOS ANGELES ANGELS OF ANAHEIM
TROPICANA FIELD, TAMPA BAY RAYS
KAUFFMAN STADIUM, KANSAS CITY ROYALS

SAFECO FIELD, SEATTLE MARINERS

OAKLAND-ALAMEDA COUNTY COLISEUM, OAKLAND ATHLETICS

BUSCH STADIUM, ST. LOUIS CARDINALS

YANKEE STADIUM, NEW YORK YANKEES
WHATEVER IT'S CALLED THIS WEEK, STADIUM, FLORIDA MARLINS
HUBERT H. HUMPHREY METRODOME, MINNESOTA TWINS

AT&T PARK, SAN FRANCISCO GIANTS

PNC PARK, PITTSBURGH PIRATES

GREAT AMERICAN BALL PARK, CINCINNATI REDS

U.S. CELLULAR FIELD, CHICAGO WHITE SOX
MILLER PARK, MILWAUKEE BREWERS
RANGERS BALLPARK IN ARLINGTON, TEXAS RANGERS

COMERICA PARK, DETROIT TIGERS

$14—1250

SMOKING
WHICH MAJOR LEAGUE BALLPARKS ALLOW IT

SMOKING AREA(S) WITHIN THE STADIUM
SMOKING AREA(S) OUTSIDE THE STADIUM
OFFICIALLY NO SMOKING, BUT IN PRACTICE, THERE IS A SMOKING AREA
NO SMOKING AND NO RE-ENTRY

Atlanta Braves
Baltimore Orioles
Colorado Rockies
Detroit Tigers
Florida Marlins
Houston Astros
Kansas City Royals
Los Angeles Angels of Anaheim
Milwaukee Brewers
Oakland Athletics
Philadelphia Phillies
Texas Rangers
Arizona Diamondbacks
Chicago White Sox
Los Angeles Dodgers
Minnesota Twins
San Diego Padres
Seattle Mariners
St. Louis Cardinals
Tampa Bay Rays
Washington Nationals
Boston Red Sox
New York Mets
Chicago Cubs
Cincinnati Reds
Cleveland Indians
New York Yankees
Pittsburgh Pirates
San Francisco Giants
Toronto Blue Jays

BALLPARK ELEVATIONS
DENVER'S QUITE HIGH UP, ISN'T IT?

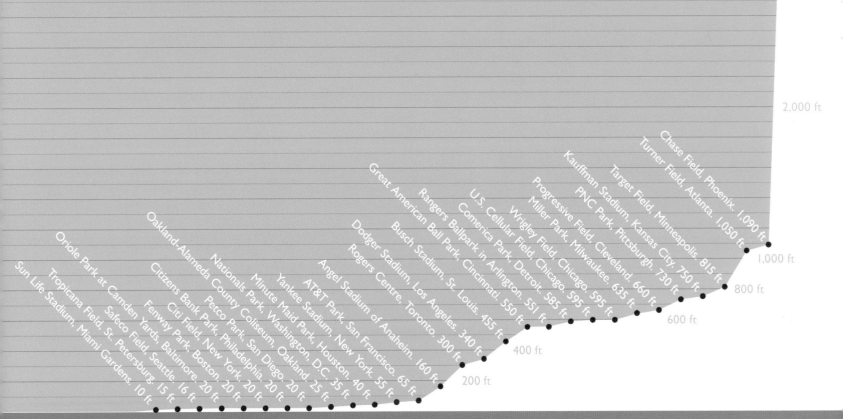

Coors Field, Denver, 5,280 ft

5,000 ft

4,000 ft

3,000 ft

2,000 ft

Chase Field, Phoenix, 1,090 ft
Turner Field, Atlanta, 1,050 ft
Kauffman Stadium, Kansas City, 750 ft
Target Field, Minneapolis, 815 ft
PNC Park, Pittsburgh, 730 ft
Progressive Field Cleveland, 660 ft
Miller Park, Milwaukee, 635 ft
Wrigley Field, Chicago, 595 ft
U.S. Cellular Field, Chicago, 595 ft
Comerica Park, Detroit, 585 ft
Rangers Ballpark in Arlington, 551 ft
Great American Ball Park, Cincinnati, 550 ft
Busch Stadium, St. Louis, 455 ft
Dodger Stadium, Los Angeles, 340 ft
Rogers Centre, Toronto, 300 ft
Angel Stadium of Anaheim, 160 ft
AT&T Park, San Francisco, 65 ft
Yankee Stadium, New York, 55 ft
Minute Maid Park, Houston, 40 ft
Nationals Park, Washington, D.C. 35 ft
Oakland-Alameda County Coliseum, Oakland, 25 ft
Petco Park, San Diego, 20 ft
Citizens Bank Park, Philadelphia, 20 ft
Citi Field, New York, 20 ft
Fenway Park, Boston, 20 ft
Oriole Park at Camden Yards, Baltimore, 20 ft
Safeco Field, Seattle, 16 ft
Tropicana Field, St. Petersburg, 15 ft
Sun Life Stadium, Miami Gardens, 10 ft

1,000 ft
800 ft
600 ft
400 ft
200 ft

UNVISITED PARKS

The same circumstances that led to spending my summer in Toronto watching the Jays and their opponents (see page 128) also kept me from visiting a great many other ballparks. Seeing the stadiums I'd yet to visit was going to be a big part of this book—an Englishman undertaking a quintessentially American sports thing, the baseball road trip. Lying in bed in my apartment in Berlin, I was feeling a wee bit melancholy about not being able to see Tropicana Field. Melancholia is a wonderful state sometimes; it's something that you can wallow in. And thanks to the magic of Google Street View I could drive around towns, skirt around the ballparks, and see the surrounding areas. I could even pay a brief visit to Turner, Montana. I couldn't, as I'd hoped, arrive in Turner with a backpack, a smile, and my English accent and subsequently charm my way into some clichéd farm girl's underpants and be run out of town by her father. But I could click on an arrow and see what sort of buildings are there, then zoom out and check out what I'm missing by not visiting Nationals Park in D.C. I'm not missing much, by the looks of the outside. Same goes for the outside of Chase Field, which from East Buchanan Street kinda looks like some sort of discount warehouse. I fly over the country in seconds, landing in Detroit and scoping out the stone tiger-head statues, each cat with a baseball in its mouth. If Google Street View could be lit like a Hollywood movie, Detroit's stadium entrance would for all the world look like something out of a baseball-themed scene in a scary movie. I leap over Lake Erie to Cleveland and check out the neighborhood, riding in an imaginary taxicab up South Broadway, looking out of the window at Jacobs Field. And, at the time of writing, there's still a Jacobs Field sign in a few of the Street View shots. One click further, though, and you are looking at Progressive Field. I'll have a little chuckle to myself thinking about a team with an offensive name

and an even more offensive logo playing in a park called *Progressive* Field. Then I climb into my imaginary car and head southwest down I-71 to Cincinnati. As I click my way around the Great American Ball Park (a name that, were it not for it being a corporate name-for-hire, would be simultaneously awesome and teeth-grindingly annoying), I turn the fan off in my room and start sweating so I can feel a bit more like I would on a July afternoon in Cincinnati. This is one of the ballparks that I most wanted to visit. That odd gap in the stands between third and home, the Power Stacks, the steamboats on the Ohio River. And either side of the ballpark, there are the 0.8 mile of West Pete Rose Way and the 0.6 mile of East Pete Rose Way. I would walk the entire distance, imagining Pete Rose late at night going back and forth along East and then West Pete Rose Way in a red 1975 Camaro, thinking about base hits and stolen bases, mimicking WLW's Marty Brennaman's calls of his triumphs, sitting in the car looking at the deserted ballpark in the early hours of the morning, falling asleep hoping for that Hall of Fame dream to happen again . . . (There's something about baseball players, I think, that really does allow you to project personalities and thoughts onto them. Maybe it's because we see close-ups of their faces on TV so much more often compared to other sports figures.) And finally I'd shoot over to Boston and look at the Street View photos clearly taken on game day. There's a line of people camped at Gate E on Lansdowne Street hoping to get game day tickets, next to the back side of the Green Monster. The Internet's great for baseball. I can see the ballparks in Street View, I can watch the games live on MLB.TV, soak up stats and history at BaseballReference.com, and read the galaxy of other blogs. But the Internet's not the same as real live baseball, and no matter how enjoyable it is to Street View my way around the United States, I'd much rather be in the line at Gate E.

TURNER, MONTANA
THE AMERICAN TOWN FARTHEST FROM A MAJOR LEAGUE TEAM

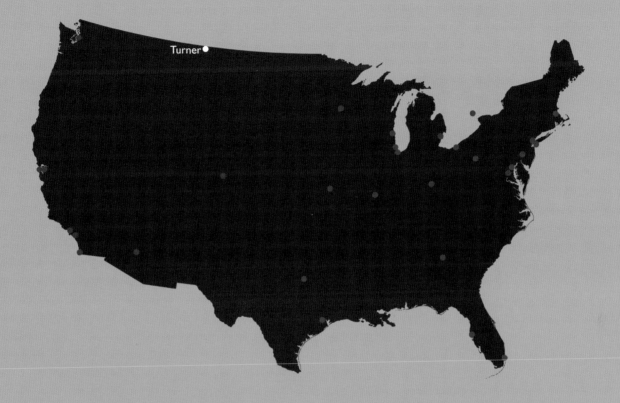

TWELVE MILES SOUTH OF THE CANADIAN BORDER, AND ABOUT FOUR HOURS' DRIVE FROM GREAT FALLS, TURNER IS THE AMERICAN TOWN (WITHIN THE CONTIGUOUS STATES) FARTHEST FROM A MAJOR LEAGUE BASEBALL TEAM. AS THE CROW FLIES, ITS NEAREST TEAM IS THE SEATTLE MARINERS, SOME 646.93 MILES AWAY. BUT LOYALTIES IN TURNER COULD BE SPLIT WITH THEIR OTHER "LOCAL" TEAM, THE COLORADO ROCKIES, WHO ARE 649.05 MILES AWAY. ACCORDING TO GOOGLE MAPS, THE DRIVE FROM TURNER TO SAFECO FIELD WOULD BE 863 MILES, AND WOULD TAKE ABOUT 14 HOURS.

Ballpark Dude

BASEBALL AND THE WAVE
A VENN DIAGRAM EXPLAINING THE RELATIONSHIP THEY SHOULD HAVE

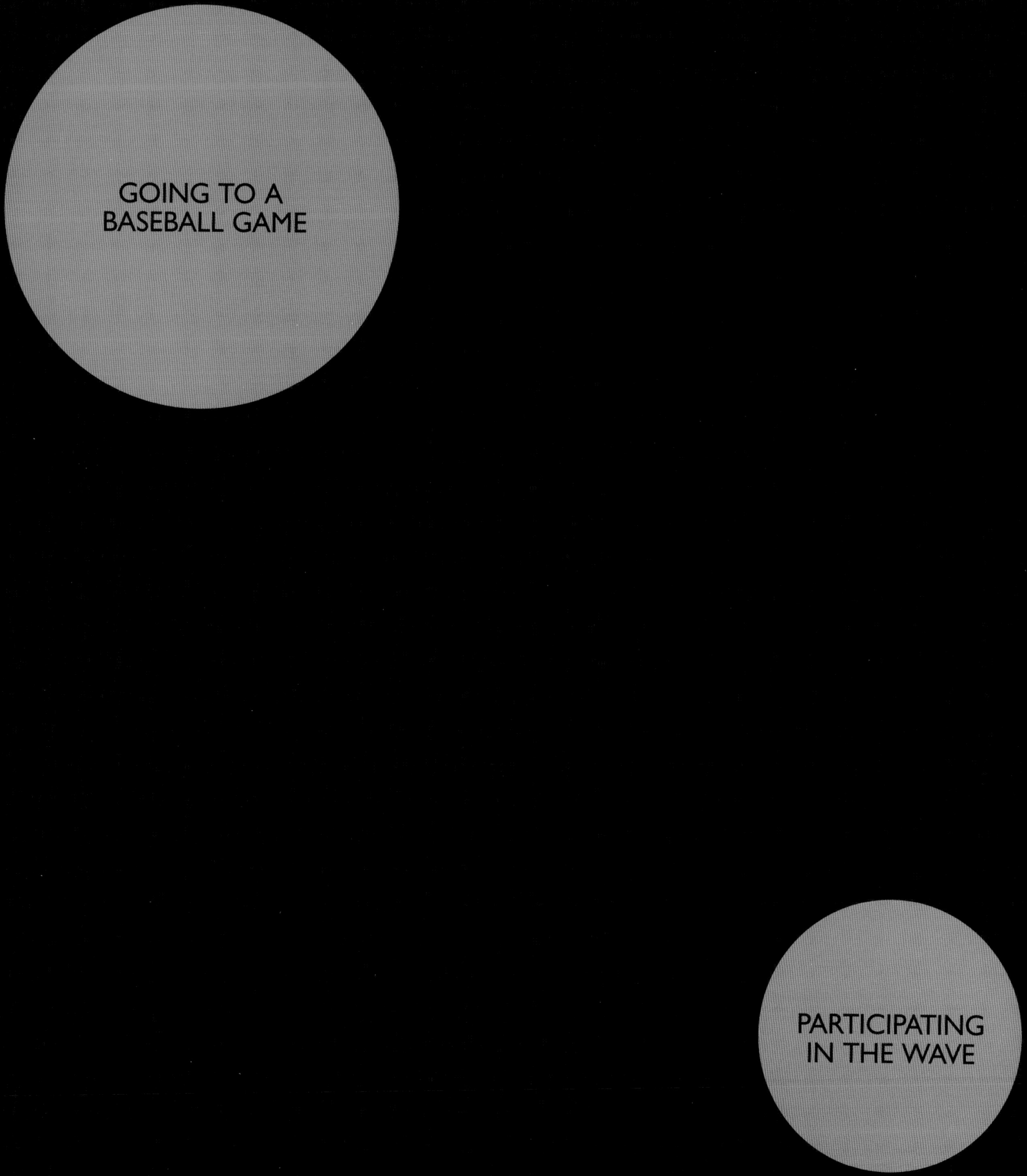

GOING TO A
BASEBALL GAME

PARTICIPATING
IN THE WAVE

GUESS THE SONG

ORIOLES 11 RED SOX 10, CAMDEN YARDS, 6/30/2009

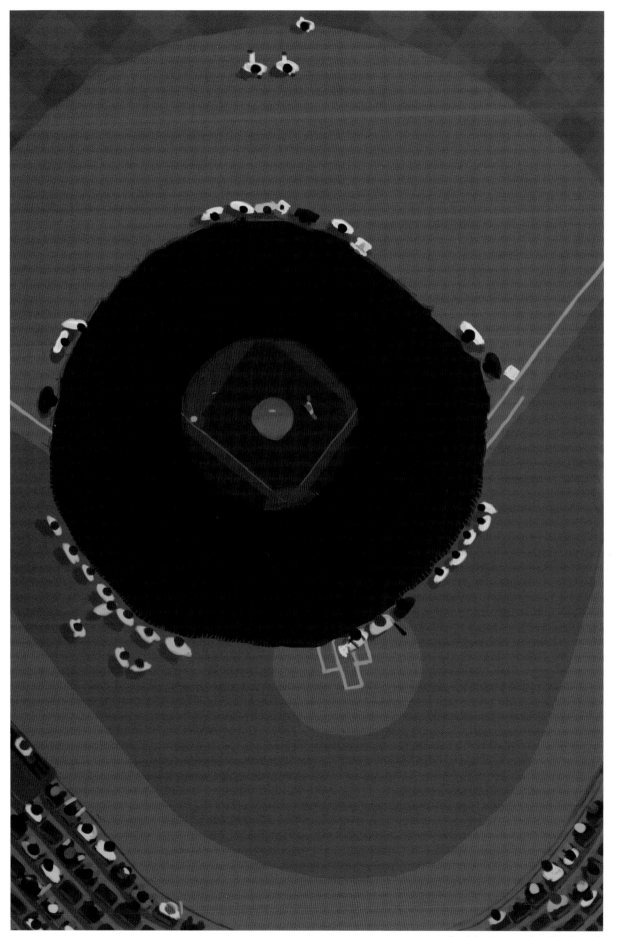

Sinkhole at the Ballpark

STARTERS VS. RELIEVERS
INNINGS PITCHED, 2009 REGULAR SEASON

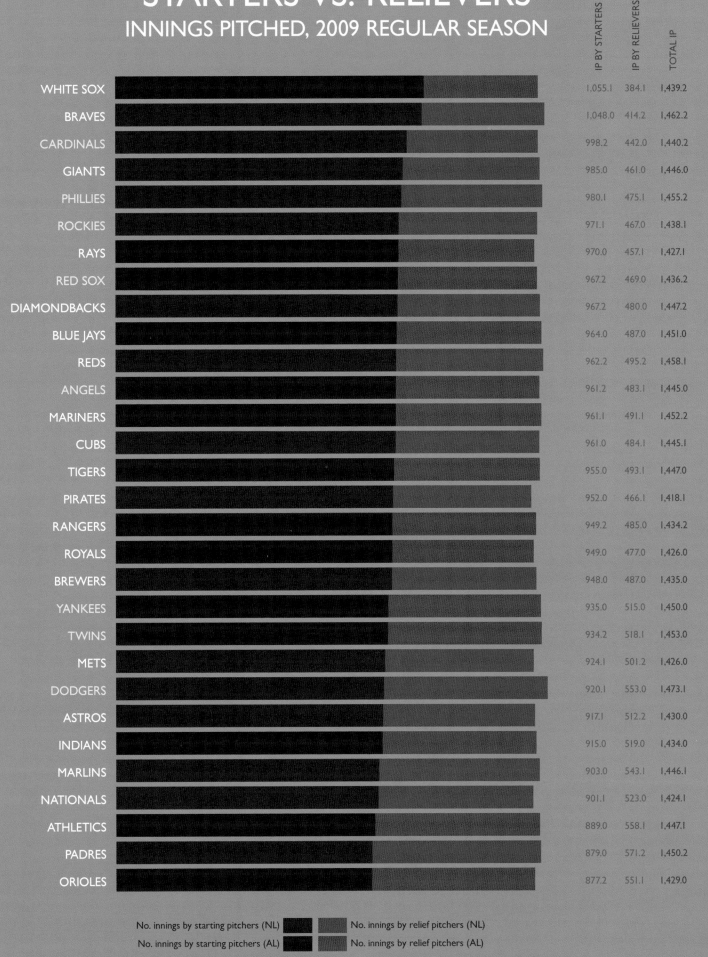

	IP BY STARTERS	IP BY RELIEVERS	TOTAL IP
WHITE SOX	1,055.1	384.1	1,439.2
BRAVES	1,048.0	414.2	1,462.2
CARDINALS	998.2	442.0	1,440.2
GIANTS	985.0	461.0	1,446.0
PHILLIES	980.1	475.1	1,455.2
ROCKIES	971.1	467.0	1,438.1
RAYS	970.0	457.1	1,427.1
RED SOX	967.2	469.0	1,436.2
DIAMONDBACKS	967.2	480.0	1,447.2
BLUE JAYS	964.0	487.0	1,451.0
REDS	962.2	495.2	1,458.1
ANGELS	961.2	483.1	1,445.0
MARINERS	961.1	491.1	1,452.2
CUBS	961.0	484.1	1,445.1
TIGERS	955.0	493.1	1,447.0
PIRATES	952.0	466.1	1,418.1
RANGERS	949.2	485.0	1,434.2
ROYALS	949.0	477.0	1,426.0
BREWERS	948.0	487.0	1,435.0
YANKEES	935.0	515.0	1,450.0
TWINS	934.2	518.1	1,453.0
METS	924.1	501.2	1,426.0
DODGERS	920.1	553.0	1,473.1
ASTROS	917.1	512.2	1,430.0
INDIANS	915.0	519.0	1,434.0
MARLINS	903.0	543.1	1,446.1
NATIONALS	901.1	523.0	1,424.1
ATHLETICS	889.0	558.1	1,447.1
PADRES	879.0	571.2	1,450.2
ORIOLES	877.2	551.1	1,429.0

No. innings by starting pitchers (NL)   No. innings by relief pitchers (NL)

No. innings by starting pitchers (AL)   No. innings by relief pitchers (AL)

Playoff teams in yellow

COMPLETE GAMES
OR THE ENORMOUS INCREASE IN RELIEF PITCHERS OVER THE YEARS

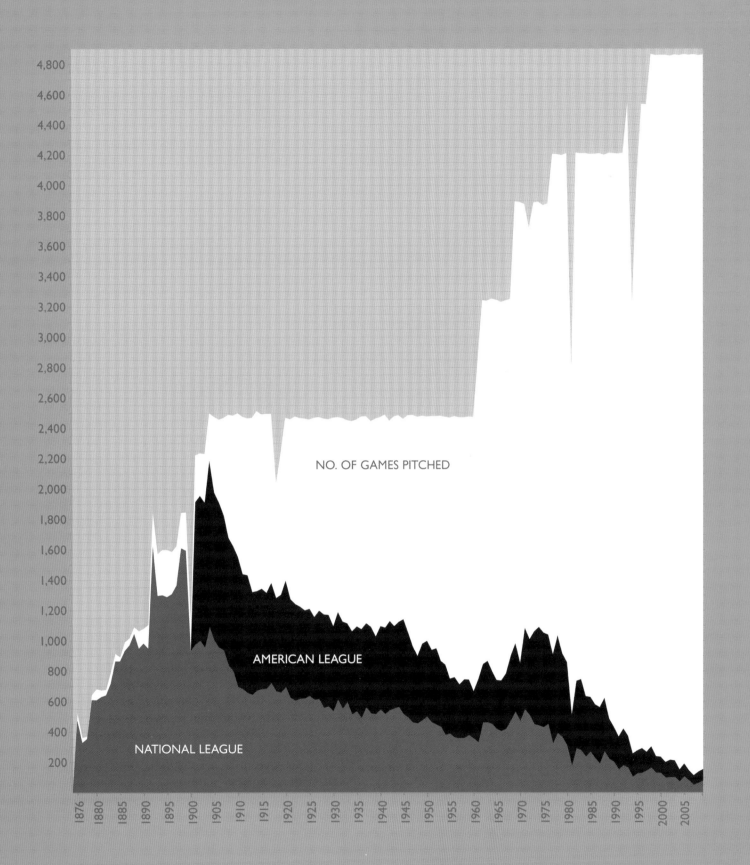

NO. OF GAMES PITCHED

AMERICAN LEAGUE

NATIONAL LEAGUE

PERFECT GAMES

Year	Pitcher	Handedness	Day/Night	Time of Game	Pitches-Strikes
1880	**LEE RICHMOND** — Cleveland Blues 0, Worcester Ruby Legs 1 — Worcester Agricultural Fairgrounds, June 12, 1880	LHP	Day	1.26	Unknown
1880	**JOHN MONTGOMERY WARD** — Providence Grays 5, Buffalo Bisons 0 — Messer Street Grounds, June 17, 1880	RHP	Day	Unknown	Unknown
1904	**CY YOUNG** — Philadelphia Athletics 0, Boston Americans 3 — Huntington Avenue Grounds, May 5, 1904	RHP	Day	1.25	Unknown
1908	**ADDIE JOSS** — Chicago White Sox 0, Cleveland Naps 1 — League Park, October 2, 1908	RHP	Day	1.32	74
1922	**CHARLIE ROBERTSON** — Chicago White Sox 2, Detroit Tigers 0 — Navin Field, April 30, 1922	RHP	Day	1.55	90
1956	**DON LARSEN** — Brooklyn Dodgers 0, New York Yankees 2 — Yankee Stadium, October 8, 1956	RHP	Day	2.06	97-71
1964	**JIM BUNNING** — Philadelphia Phillies 6, New York Mets 0 — Shea Stadium, June 21, 1964	RHP	Day	2.19	90
1965	**SANDY KOUFAX** — Chicago Cubs 0, Los Angeles Dodgers 1 — Dodger Stadium, September 9, 1965	LHP	Night	1.43	113
1968	**CATFISH HUNTER** — Minnesota Twins 0, Oakland Athletics 4 — Oakland-Alameda County Coliseum, May 8, 1968	RHP	Night	2.28	107
1981	**LEN BARKER** — Toronto Blue Jays 0, Cleveland Indians 3 — Cleveland Stadium, May 15, 1981	RHP	Night	2.09	103
1984	**MIKE WITT** — California Angels 1, Texas Rangers 0 — Arlington Stadium, September 30, 1984	RHP	Day	1.49	94
1988	**TOM BROWNING** — Los Angeles Dodgers 0, Cincinnati Reds 1 — Riverfront Stadium, September 16, 1988	LHP	Night	1.51	100-72
1991	**DENNIS MARTINEZ** — Montreal Expos 2, Los Angeles Dodgers 0 — Dodger Stadium, July 28, 1991	RHP	Day	2.14	96-66
1994	**KENNY ROGERS** — California Angels 0, Texas Rangers 4 — The Ballpark in Arlington, July 28, 1994	LHP	Night	2.08	98-64
1998	**DAVID WELLS** — Minnesota Twins 0, New York Yankees 4 — Yankee Stadium, May 17, 1998	LHP	Day	2.40	120-79
1999	**DAVID CONE** — Montreal Expos 0, New York Yankees 6 — Yankee Stadium, July 18, 1999	RHP	Day	2.16	88-68
2004	**RANDY JOHNSON** — Arizona Diamondbacks 2, Atlanta Braves 0 — Turner Field, May 18, 2004	LHP	Night	2.13	117-87
2009	**MARK BUEHRLE** — Tampa Bay Rays 0, Chicago White Sox 5 — U.S. Cellular Field, July 23, 2009	LHP	Day	2.03	116-76
2010	**DALLAS BRADEN** — Tampa Bay Rays 0, Oakland Athletics 4 — Oakland-Alameda County Coliseum, May 9, 2010	LHP	Day	2.07	109-77
2010	**ROY HALLADAY** — Philadelphia Phillies 1, Florida Marlins 0 — Sun Life Stadium, May 29, 2010	RHP	Night	2.13	115-72
2010	**ARMANDO GALARRAGA (ASTERISK)** — Cleveland Indians 0, Detroit Tigers 3 — Comerica Park, June 2, 2010	RHP	Night	1.41	83-67

HANDEDNESS

DAY OR NIGHT

TIME OF GAME

PITCHES-STRIKES
(SOME STRIKE DATA NOT KNOWN)

STRIKEOUTS
GROUND BALLS
FLY BALLS
(SOME DATA NOT KNOWN)

AGE	SEASONS OF MLB SERVICE AND POINT AT WHICH PERFECT GAME OCCURED	PREVIOUS COMPLETE GAMES	PREVIOUS SHUTOUTS	PREVIOUS NO-HITTERS	OPPONENT'S W-L% PRIOR TO THE GAME	HOME OR ROAD GAME	ATTENDANCE	LEAGUE
23		≥1	≥0	0	.571	home	Unknown	NL
20		≥95	≥8	0	.320	road	Unknown	NL
37		≥537	≥48	1	.538	home	10,267	AL
28		≥199	39	0	.578	home	10,598	AL
26		1	0	0	.286	road	25,000	AL
27		30	5	0	.604	home	64,519	AL
32		82	18	0	.308	road	32,026	NL
29		107	31	1	.461	home	29,139	NL
22		21	7	3	.542	home	6,298	AL
25		13	3	0	.323	home	7,290	AL
24		22	3	0	.431	road	8,375	NL
28		16	7	0	.583	home	16,591	NL
36		98	21	0	.583	road	45,560	NL
29		10	1	0	.412	home	46,581	AL
34		22	3	0	.439	home	49,820	AL
36		56	21	0	.379	home	41,930	IL
40		104	38	1	.472	road	23,381	NL
30	(active)	24	7	1	.495	home	28,036	AL
26	(active)	0	0	0	.733	home	12,228	AL
33	(active)	53	17	0	.490	road	"25,086"	NL
28	(active)	0	0	0	.380	home	17,738	AL

DON'T MENTION IT
HOW SOON DID TV BROADCASTERS MENTION A NO-NO?

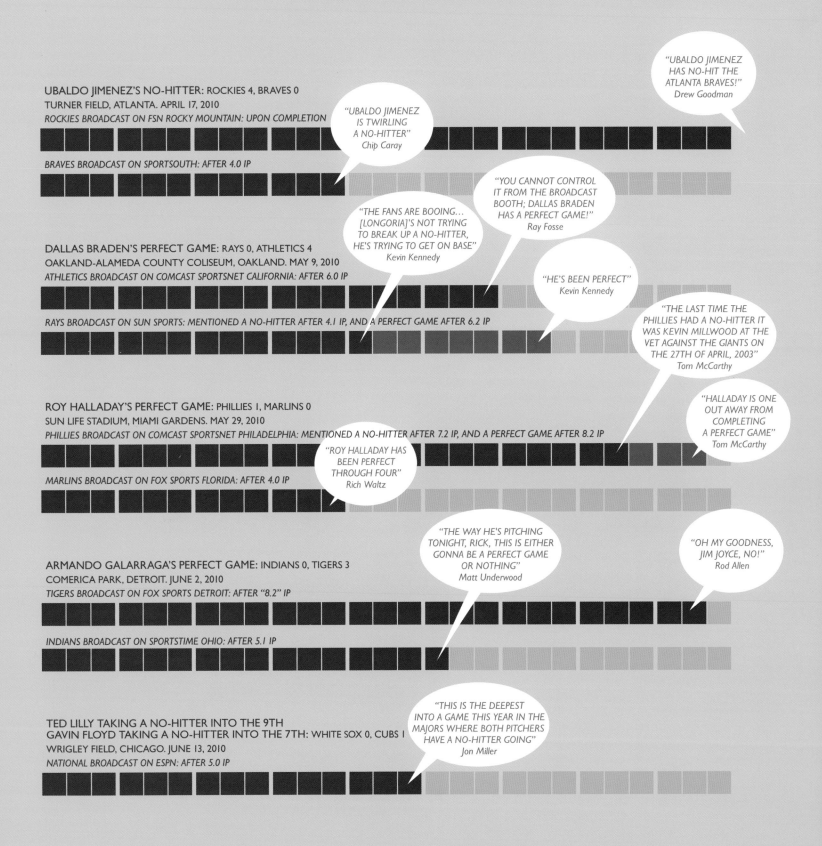

UBALDO JIMENEZ'S NO-HITTER: ROCKIES 4, BRAVES 0
TURNER FIELD, ATLANTA. APRIL 17, 2010
ROCKIES BROADCAST ON FSN ROCKY MOUNTAIN: UPON COMPLETION

"UBALDO JIMENEZ IS TWIRLING A NO-HITTER"
Chip Caray

"UBALDO JIMENEZ HAS NO-HIT THE ATLANTA BRAVES!"
Drew Goodman

BRAVES BROADCAST ON SPORTSOUTH: AFTER 4.0 IP

"THE FANS ARE BOOING... [LONGORIA]'S NOT TRYING TO BREAK UP A NO-HITTER, HE'S TRYING TO GET ON BASE"
Kevin Kennedy

"YOU CANNOT CONTROL IT FROM THE BROADCAST BOOTH; DALLAS BRADEN HAS A PERFECT GAME!"
Ray Fosse

DALLAS BRADEN'S PERFECT GAME: RAYS 0, ATHLETICS 4
OAKLAND-ALAMEDA COUNTY COLISEUM, OAKLAND. MAY 9, 2010
ATHLETICS BROADCAST ON COMCAST SPORTSNET CALIFORNIA: AFTER 6.0 IP

"HE'S BEEN PERFECT"
Kevin Kennedy

"THE LAST TIME THE PHILLIES HAD A NO-HITTER IT WAS KEVIN MILLWOOD AT THE VET AGAINST THE GIANTS ON THE 27TH OF APRIL, 2003"
Tom McCarthy

RAYS BROADCAST ON SUN SPORTS: MENTIONED A NO-HITTER AFTER 4.1 IP, AND A PERFECT GAME AFTER 6.2 IP

"HALLADAY IS ONE OUT AWAY FROM COMPLETING A PERFECT GAME"
Tom McCarthy

ROY HALLADAY'S PERFECT GAME: PHILLIES 1, MARLINS 0
SUN LIFE STADIUM, MIAMI GARDENS. MAY 29, 2010
PHILLIES BROADCAST ON COMCAST SPORTSNET PHILADELPHIA: MENTIONED A NO-HITTER AFTER 7.2 IP, AND A PERFECT GAME AFTER 8.2 IP

"ROY HALLADAY HAS BEEN PERFECT THROUGH FOUR"
Rich Waltz

MARLINS BROADCAST ON FOX SPORTS FLORIDA: AFTER 4.0 IP

"THE WAY HE'S PITCHING TONIGHT, RICK, THIS IS EITHER GONNA BE A PERFECT GAME OR NOTHING"
Matt Underwood

"OH MY GOODNESS, JIM JOYCE, NO!"
Rod Allen

ARMANDO GALARRAGA'S PERFECT GAME: INDIANS 0, TIGERS 3
COMERICA PARK, DETROIT. JUNE 2, 2010
TIGERS BROADCAST ON FOX SPORTS DETROIT: AFTER "8.2" IP

INDIANS BROADCAST ON SPORTSTIME OHIO: AFTER 5.1 IP

"THIS IS THE DEEPEST INTO A GAME THIS YEAR IN THE MAJORS WHERE BOTH PITCHERS HAVE A NO-HITTER GOING"
Jon Miller

TED LILLY TAKING A NO-HITTER INTO THE 9TH
GAVIN FLOYD TAKING A NO-HITTER INTO THE 7TH: WHITE SOX 0, CUBS 1
WRIGLEY FIELD, CHICAGO. JUNE 13, 2010
NATIONAL BROADCAST ON ESPN: AFTER 5.0 IP

If a no-hitter or perfect game was alluded to but not explicitly mentioned (that is, the announcer did not refer to a "no-hitter," "no-no," "perfect game," or the pitcher's perfection), I've ignored it in this analysis. Personally, I'm not superstitious, but I kind of like it when a broadcaster makes the effort to be a bit more creative than blurting it out after every other pitch. I'm looking at you, Waltz.

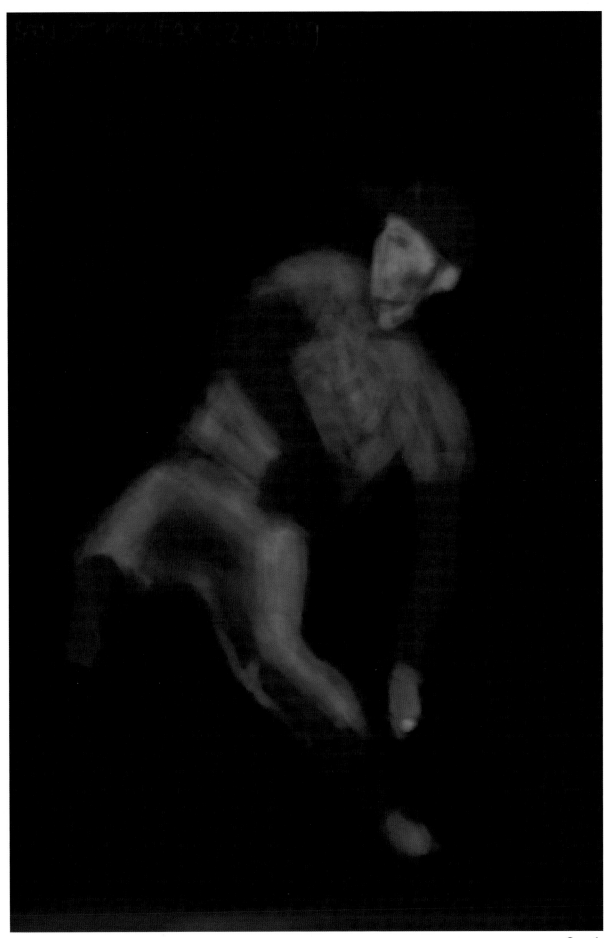

Sandy

716,083 PITCHES
ST. LOUIS TO MUMBAI

Adding together all the pitches thrown by all the pitchers of all the Major League Baseball teams during the 2006 season (including the postseason). Imagine if all of those pitches were made in one continuous line. The 716,083 pitches thrown during 2006—measured from the rubber to home plate—equal just over 8,318.5 miles; or the distance from the rubber at Busch Stadium, St. Louis, to the beach of Uran township, just south of Mumbai, India.

LEFTIES, RIGHTIES, & SWITCHIES
NUMBER OF EACH ON OPENING DAY 2009 ACTIVE ROSTERS

PITCHERS

LEFT-HANDED PITCHERS WHO HIT LEFT-HANDED: 85
LEFT-HANDED PITCHERS WHO SWITCH-HIT: 1
LEFT-HANDED PITCHERS WHO HIT RIGHT-HANDED: 14
RIGHT-HANDED PITCHERS WHO HIT LEFT-HANDED: 21
RIGHT-HANDED PITCHERS WHO SWITCH-HIT: 3
RIGHT-HANDED PITCHERS WHO HIT RIGHT-HANDED: 233

POSITION PLAYERS

LEFT-HANDED HITTERS WHO THROW LEFT-HANDED: 51
LEFT-HANDED HITTERS WHO THROW RIGHT-HANDED: 69
SWITCH HITTERS WHO THROW LEFT-HANDED: 3
SWITCH HITTERS WHO THROW RIGHT-HANDED: 63
RIGHT-HANDED HITTERS WHO THROW LEFT-HANDED: 2
RIGHT-HANDED HITTERS WHO THROW RIGHT-HANDED: 204

BASERUNNING
WHAT DISTANCE IS COVERED IN A SEASON?

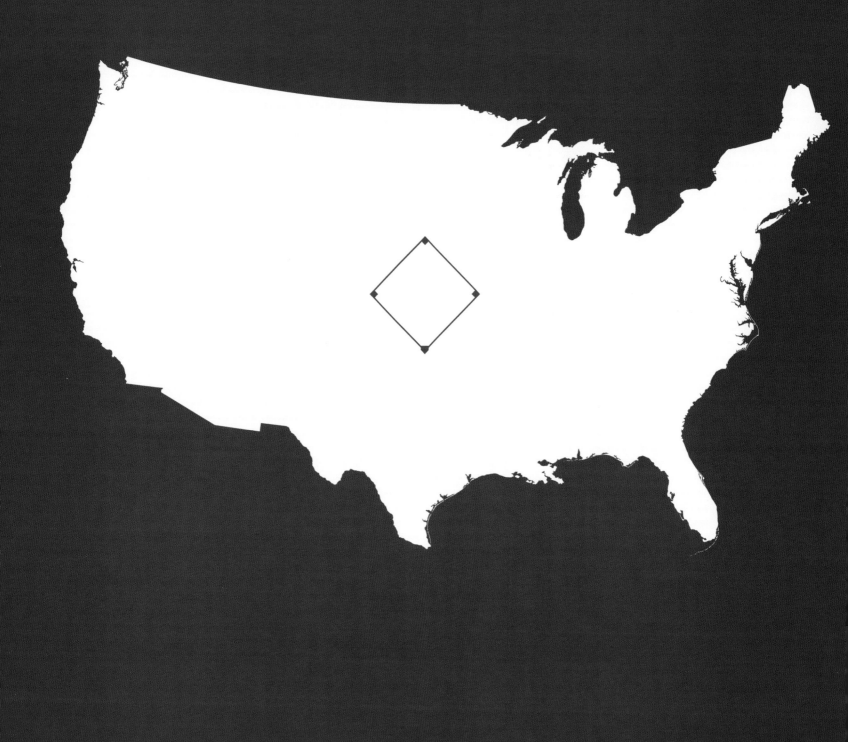

All the bases run by all the players of all the Major League Baseball teams during the 2009 season total 69,285.
Multiply that by 90 feet and you've got a distance of 1,181 miles.
The diamond above is how big a baseball diamond would be if the base paths totaled 1,181 miles. It's also
more or less the distance, as the crow flies, from Camden Yards, Baltimore, to Rangers Ballpark, Arlington.

STOLEN BASES
IF PLAYERS ACTUALLY STOLE THE BASES…

MAJOR LEAGUE BASEBALL USES SCHUTT "JACK CORBETT HOLLYWOOD BASES."
ONE OF THESE BASES (WITHOUT THE ANCHOR) COSTS $89.99 AT MODELL'S. *

THERE WERE 2,757 STOLEN BASES DURING THE 2008 MLB SEASON.
IF THE BASES WERE *ACTUALLY* STOLEN, MLB TEAMS WOULD HAVE LOST BASES WORTH $248,102.43.

WILLY TAVERAS (COLORADO ROCKIES) WAS THE LEAGUE LEADER IN 2008 WITH 68 STOLEN BASES.
THAT'S $6,119.32 TOTAL VALUE. UNDER COLORADO LAW, THAT'S A CLASS 4 FELONY.

* PRICE CHECKED IN JUNE 2009

200,000 BASEBALLS
ONE SEASON'S WORTH OF BASEBALLS

MAJOR LEAGUE BASEBALL USES AROUND 200,000 BASEBALLS DURING A SEASON. IF THEY WERE LAID OUT FLAT ON THE GROUND, INTERLOCKING LIKE A HONEYCOMB, THEY WOULD COVER 8,118.75 SQUARE FEET. THAT'S JUST A FEW SQUARE FEET LARGER THAN THE SPACE BETWEEN THE BASES. WHICH KIND OF BLOWS MY MIND A LITTLE BIT.

SURNAMES

THE MOST COMMON SURNAMES IN THE MAJORS (1871-2009)

YEAR-BY-YEAR OCCURRENCE OF EACH SURNAME

Count	Surname
145	SMITH
104	JOHNSON
95	JONES
84	MILLER
80	BROWN
73	WILLIAMS
69	WILSON
63	DAVIS
49	MOORE
47	TAYLOR
42	ANDERSON
42	THOMPSON
41	MURPHY
40	CLARK
40	SULLIVAN
40	WHITE
39	THOMAS
39	WALKER
39	YOUNG
37	MARTINEZ
36	HERNANDEZ
36	RODRIGUEZ
36	WRIGHT
34	JACKSON
32	BAKER
32	HARRIS
31	GONZALEZ
31	MARTIN
30	ROBINSON
29	ALLEN
29	KELLY
28	ADAMS
28	GARCIA
27	BELL
27	LEE
26	PHILLIPS
25	FISHER
25	HALL
25	PEREZ
25	SCOTT

1880 1890 1900 1910 1920 1930 1940 1950 1960 1970 1980 1990 2000

BORN IN THE U.S.A.

OR DOMINICAN REPUBLIC, PUERTO RICO, VENEZUELA, JAPAN, AUSTRALIA...

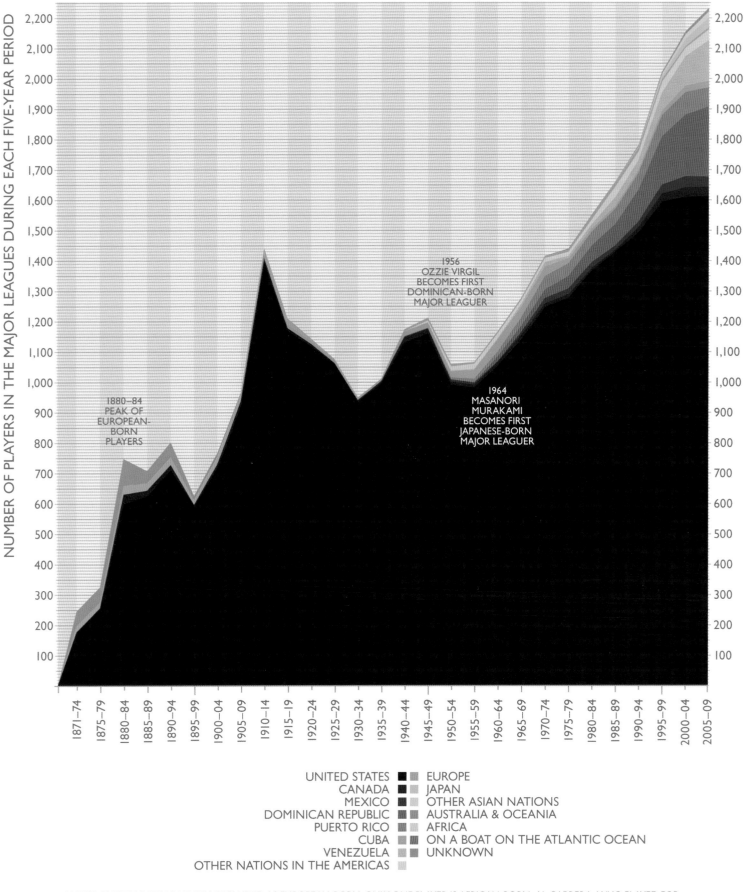

NUMBER OF PLAYERS IN THE MAJOR LEAGUES DURING EACH FIVE-YEAR PERIOD

1880–84
PEAK OF
EUROPEAN-
BORN
PLAYERS

1956
OZZIE VIRGIL
BECOMES FIRST
DOMINICAN-BORN
MAJOR LEAGUER

1964
MASANORI
MURAKAMI
BECOMES FIRST
JAPANESE-BORN
MAJOR LEAGUER

UNITED STATES
CANADA
MEXICO
DOMINICAN REPUBLIC
PUERTO RICO
CUBA
VENEZUELA
OTHER NATIONS IN THE AMERICAS

EUROPE
JAPAN
OTHER ASIAN NATIONS
AUSTRALIA & OCEANIA
AFRICA
ON A BOAT ON THE ATLANTIC OCEAN
UNKNOWN

NOTES: PLAYERS BORN IN RUSSIA INCLUDED AS EUROPEAN-BORN. ONLY ONE PLAYER IS AFRICAN-BORN: AL CABRERA, WHO PLAYED FOR
THE 1913 CARDINALS, WAS BORN IN THE SPANISH-RULED CANARY ISLANDS, WHICH IS JUST 62 MILES WEST OF WESTERN SAHARA.
ED PORRAY, WHO PITCHED 3 GAMES FOR THE 1914 BUFFALO BUFFEDS, WAS BORN ON A SHIP ON THE ATLANTIC OCEAN.

ED PORRAY
BORN AT SEA, ON THE ATLANTIC OCEAN. DECEMBER 5, 1888

ED PORRAY PITCHED 10.1 INNINGS OVER THREE GAMES IN 1914 FOR THE BUFFALO BUFFEDS OF THE FEDERAL LEAGUE. HE GAVE UP 18 HITS, 2 HOME RUNS, 7 WALKS, AND 9 RUNS (5 EARNED). HE DIED ON JULY 13, 1954, IN LACKAWAXEN, PENNSYLVANIA.

ARIZONA
BASEBALL HEAVEN

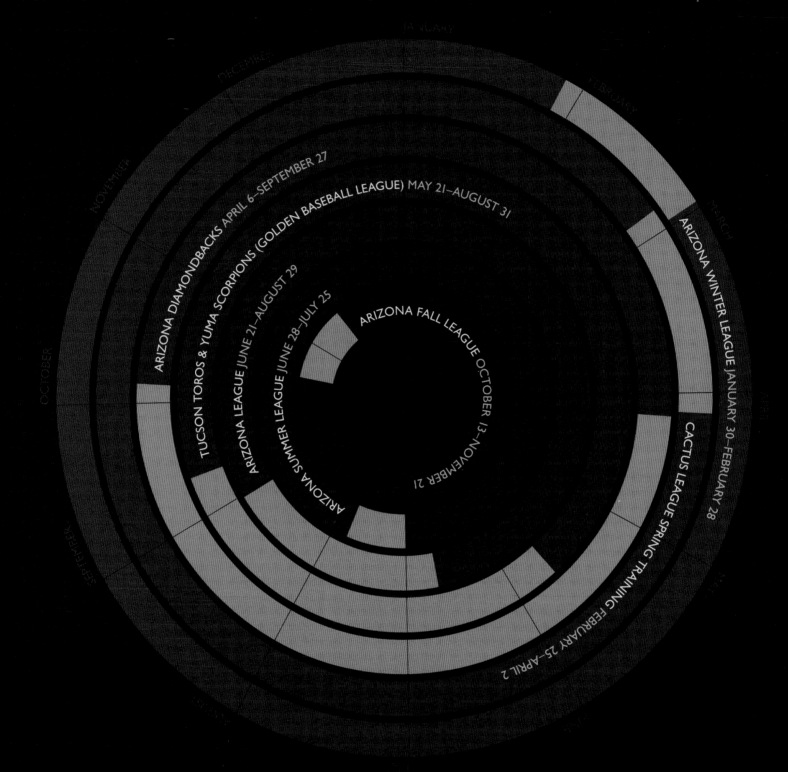

Should you have a car, a fairly substantial amount of disposable income, and lots and lots of free time, Arizona would be a good place for a baseball fan to live. There's the major league Arizona Diamondbacks, Cactus League spring training, Arizona League rookie ball, and a chance to see some top prospects in the Arizona Fall League. The independent Golden Baseball league also has two teams in Arizona, and a couple of short season leagues, the Arizona Winter League and Arizona Summer League.

The above chart looks at baseball in Arizona in 2009. There were 877 games in the state. 712 of those were in the Phoenix Metropolitan Area.
You could've seen a live game in the Phoenix Metropolitan Area on 197 days of the year. And if you were willing to drive to Tucson or Yuma, you could've seen live baseball on an additional 36 days.

December and most of January would've been hellishly boring, though.

HOMOSEXUALITY
IN THE MAJOR LEAGUES

EVERY SQUARE REPRESENTS ONE MAJOR LEAGUE PLAYER.

GLENN BURKE, WHO PLAYED FOR THE DODGERS (1976–78) AND ATHLETICS (1978–79), IS, TO DATE, THE ONLY OPENLY GAY MAJOR LEAGUE PLAYER. HE ALSO HELPED POPULARIZE THE HIGH FIVE: HIS HAND AND DUSTY BAKER'S HAND WERE THE FIRST TO HIGH-FIVE IN BASEBALL. HE DIED FROM AIDS-RELATED COMPLICATIONS IN 1995 AT THE AGE OF 42. BILLY BEAN (NOT BILLY BEANE) CAME OUT FOUR YEARS AFTER HIS CAREER ENDED. EVERYONE ELSE IS EITHER HETEROSEXUAL OR NOT TELLING.

OVERALL STRENGTH OF MLB TEAMS

1995–2010

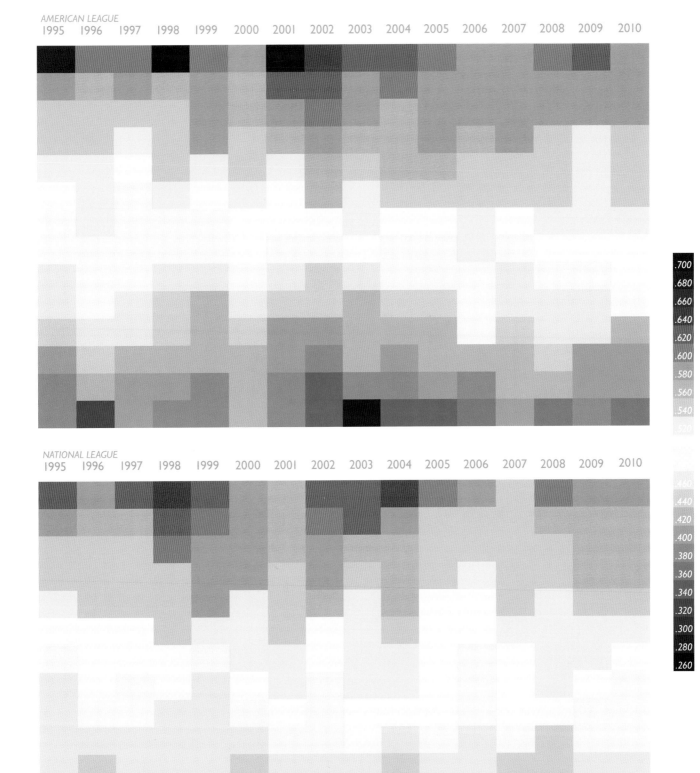

100-WIN SEASONS

CHICAGO CUBS *1906* 116–36
SEATTLE MARINERS *2001* 116–46
NEW YORK YANKEES *1998* 114–48
CLEVELAND INDIANS *1954* 111–43
PITTSBURGH PIRATES *1909* 110–42
NEW YORK YANKEES *1927* 110–44
NEW YORK YANKEES *1961* 109–53
BALTIMORE ORIOLES *1969* 109–53
NEW YORK METS *1986* 108–54
CINCINNATI REDS *1975* 108–54
BALTIMORE ORIOLES *1970* 108–54
PHILADELPHIA ATHLETICS *1931* 107–45
CHICAGO CUBS *1907* 107–45
NEW YORK YANKEES *1932* 107–47
NEW YORK YANKEES *1939* 106–45
NEW YORK GIANTS *1904* 106–47
ST. LOUIS CARDINALS *1942* 106–48
ATLANTA BRAVES *1998* 106–56
BOSTON RED SOX *1912* 105–47
NEW YORK GIANTS *1905* 105–48
ST. LOUIS CARDINALS *1943* 105–49
ST. LOUIS CARDINALS *1944* 105–49
BROOKLYN DODGERS *1953* 105–49
ST. LOUIS CARDINALS *2004* 105–57
PHILADELPHIA ATHLETICS *1929* 104–46
CHICAGO CUBS *1909* 104–49
CHICAGO CUBS *1910* 104–50
BROOKLYN DODGERS *1942* 104–50
BOSTON RED SOX *1946* 104–50
NEW YORK YANKEES *1963* 104–57
DETROIT TIGERS *1984* 104–58
OAKLAND ATHLETICS *1988* 104–58
ATLANTA BRAVES *1993* 104–58
PITTSBURGH PIRATES *1902* 103–36
NEW YORK GIANTS *1912* 103–48
NEW YORK YANKEES *1942* 103–51
NEW YORK YANKEES *1954* 103–51
NEW YORK YANKEES *2002* 103–58
DETROIT TIGERS *1968* 103–59
NEW YORK YANKEES *1980* 103–59
OAKLAND ATHLETICS *1990* 103–59
SAN FRANCISCO GIANTS *1993* 103–59
ATLANTA BRAVES *1999* 103–59
OAKLAND ATHLETICS *2002* 103–59
NEW YORK YANKEES *2009* 103–59
SAN FRANCISCO GIANTS *1962* 103–62
BOSTON BEANEATERS *1898* 102–47
BOSTON BEANEATERS *1892* 102–48
PHILADELPHIA ATHLETICS *1910* 102–48
NEW YORK YANKEES *1936* 102–51
PHILADELPHIA ATHLETICS *1930* 102–52
NEW YORK YANKEES *1937* 102–52
BALTIMORE ORIOLES *1979* 102–57
MINNESOTA TWINS *1965* 102–60
CINCINNATI REDS *1970* 102–60
LOS ANGELES DODGERS *1974* 102–60
CINCINNATI REDS *1976* 102–60
KANSAS CITY ROYALS *1977* 102–60
HOUSTON ASTROS *1998* 102–60
OAKLAND ATHLETICS *2001* 102–60
LOS ANGELES DODGERS *1962* 102–63
BROOKLYN SUPERBAS *1899* 101–47
PHILADELPHIA ATHLETICS *1911* 101–50
BOSTON RED SOX *1915* 101–50
NEW YORK GIANTS *1913* 101–51
NEW YORK YANKEES *1928* 101–53
ST. LOUIS CARDINALS *1931* 101–53
DETROIT TIGERS *1934* 101–53
NEW YORK YANKEES *1941* 101–53
BALTIMORE ORIOLES *1971* 101–57
ATLANTA BRAVES *2002* 101–59
ST. LOUIS CARDINALS *1967* 101–60
OAKLAND ATHLETICS *1971* 101–60
DETROIT TIGERS *1961* 101–61
PHILADELPHIA PHILLIES *1976* 101–61
PHILADELPHIA PHILLIES *1977* 101–61
ST. LOUIS CARDINALS *1985* 101–61
ATLANTA BRAVES *1997* 101–61
ATLANTA BRAVES *2003* 101–61
NEW YORK YANKEES *2003* 101–62
NEW YORK YANKEES *2004* 101–61
CLEVELAND INDIANS *1995* 100–44
CINCINNATI REDS *1940* 100–53
DETROIT TIGERS *1915* 100–54
CHICAGO WHITE SOX *1917* 100–54
CHICAGO CUBS *1935* 100–54
BROOKLYN DODGERS *1941* 100–54
NEW YORK METS *1988* 100–60
SAN FRANCISCO GIANTS *2003* 100–61
NEW YORK METS *1969* 100–62
NEW YORK YANKEES *1977* 100–62
BALTIMORE ORIOLES *1980* 100–62
ARIZONA DIAMONDBACKS *1999* 100–62
ST. LOUIS CARDINALS *2005* 100–62
LOS ANGELES ANGELS OF ANAHEIM *2008* 100–62
NEW YORK YANKEES *1978* 100–63

Won World Series
Won pennant
Lost Championship Series
Lost Division Series
Did not reach playoffs

The 1898 Beaneaters, 1899 Superbas, 1902 Pirates, and 1904 Giants won the NL pennant, but there were no World Series any of those years. The 1892 Beaneaters beat the Cleveland Spiders in the exhibition World Championship series.

Eight current franchises have yet to have 100-win seasons:
Toronto Blue Jays (best: 99–62 in 1985)
San Diego Padres (98–64 in 1998)
Tampa Bay Rays (97–65 in 2008)
Milwaukee Brewers (95–66 in 1979)
Texas Rangers (95–67 in 1999)
Florida Marlins (92–70 in 1997)
Colorado Rockies (92–70 in 2009)
Washington Nationals (81–81 in 2005, although as the Montreal Expos there was a 95–65 season in 1979)

THE BEST RECORD IN BASEBALL
HOW OFTEN DOES THE BEST TEAM WIN THE WORLD SERIES?

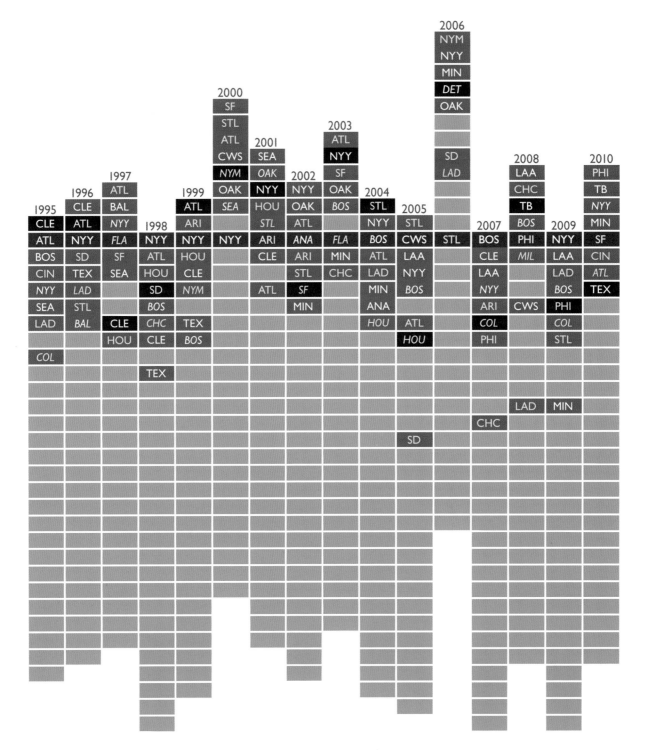

The pink boxes show the World Series winners. Teams above that line had a better regular-season record than the champions. Beige boxes show playoff teams, purple shows World Series losers. NL teams in yellow, AL teams in white. Italics for wild card teams. Joined-together boxes means those teams in the boxes had the same regular-season record (I've done this only for the playoff teams).

Some interesting stuff: the team with the best record has won only thrice (1998, 2007, and 2009); the top two teams have met only once in the World Series (1995); the top eight teams have been the playoff teams four times (1996, 2002, 2004, and 2010); the playoff team with the worst record has won the World Series twice (2000 and 2006); there was just one World Series between wild card teams (2002); all division winners had a better record than their league's wild card team in 1999; all AL playoff teams had better records than all NL playoff teams in 2007; and only once has a wild card team had the second-best record in baseball (2001)

THE BIGGEST PAYROLL IN BASEBALL

HOW OFTEN DOES THE MOST EXPENSIVE TEAM WIN THE WORLD SERIES?

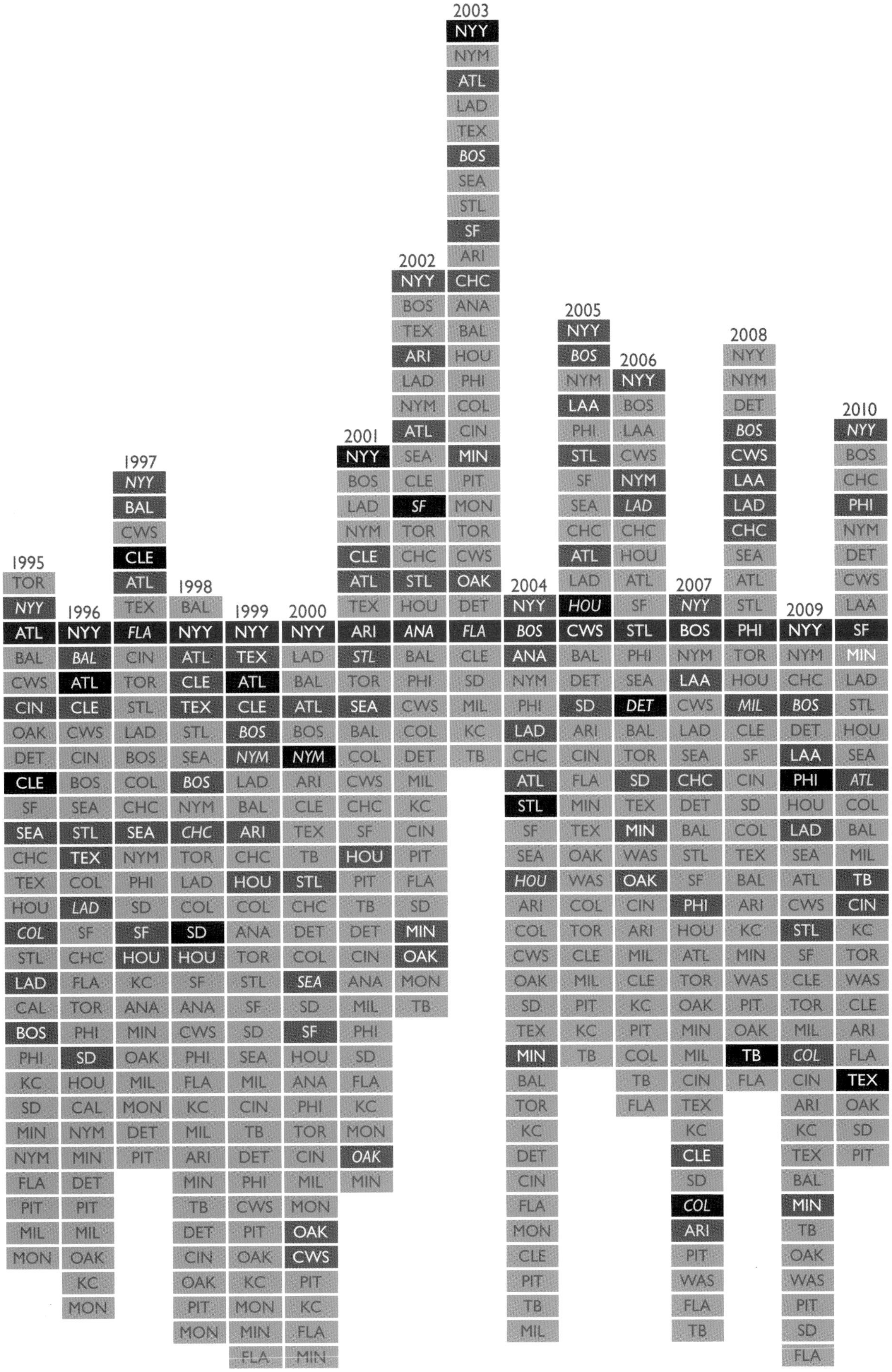
1995 TOR NYY ATL BAL CWS CIN OAK DET CLE SF SEA CHC TEX HOU COL STL LAD CAL BOS PHI KC SD MIN NYM FLA PIT MIL MON
1996 NYY BAL ATL CLE CWS CIN BOS SEA STL TEX COL LAD SF CHC FLA TOR PHI SD HOU CAL NYM MIN DET PIT MIL OAK KC MON
1997 NYY BAL CWS CLE ATL TEX FLA CIN TOR STL LAD BOS COL CHC SEA NYM PHI SD SF HOU KC ANA MIN OAK MIL MON DET PIT
1998 BAL NYY ATL CLE TEX STL SEA BOS NYM CHC TOR LAD COL SD HOU SF ANA CWS PHI FLA KC MIL ARI MIN TB DET CIN OAK PIT MON
1999 NYY TEX ATL CLE BOS NYM LAD BAL ARI CHC HOU COL ANA TOR STL SF SD SEA MIL CIN TB DET PHI CWS PIT OAK KC MON MIN FLA
2000 NYY LAD BAL ATL BOS NYM ARI CLE TEX TB STL CHC DET COL SEA SD SF HOU ANA PHI TOR CIN MIL MON OAK CWS PIT KC FLA MIN
2001 NYY BOS LAD NYM CLE ATL TEX ARI STL TOR SEA BAL COL CWS CHC SF HOU PIT TB DET CIN ANA MIL PHI SD FLA KC MON OAK MIN
2002 NYY BOS TEX ARI LAD NYM ATL SEA CLE SF TOR CHC STL HOU ANA BAL PHI CWS COL DET MIL KC CIN PIT FLA SD MIN OAK MON TB
2003 NYY NYM ATL LAD TEX BOS SEA STL SF ARI CHC ANA BAL HOU PHI COL CIN MIN PIT MON TOR CWS OAK DET FLA CLE SD MIL KC TB
2004 NYY BOS ANA NYM PHI LAD CHC ATL STL SF SEA HOU ARI COL CWS OAK SD TEX MIN BAL TOR KC DET CIN FLA MON CLE PIT TB MIL
2005 NYY BOS NYM LAA PHI STL SF SEA CHC ATL LAD HOU CWS BAL DET SD ARI CIN FLA MIN TEX OAK WAS COL TOR CLE MIL PIT KC TB
2006 NYY BOS LAA CWS NYM LAD CHC HOU ATL SF STL PHI SEA DET BAL TOR SD TEX MIN WAS OAK CIN ARI MIL CLE KC PIT COL TB FLA
2007 NYY BOS NYM LAA CWS LAD SEA CHC DET BAL STL SF PHI HOU ATL TOR OAK MIN MIL CIN TEX KC CLE SD COL ARI PIT WAS FLA TB
2008 NYY NYM DET BOS CWS LAA LAD CHC SEA ATL STL PHI TOR HOU MIL CLE SF CIN SD COL TEX BAL ARI KC MIN WAS PIT OAK TB FLA
2009 NYY NYM CHC BOS DET LAA PHI HOU LAD SEA ATL CWS STL SF CLE TOR MIL COL CIN ARI KC TEX BAL MIN TB OAK WAS PIT SD FLA
2010 NYY BOS CHC PHI NYM DET CWS LAA SF MIN LAD STL HOU SEA ATL COL BAL MIL TB CIN KC TOR WAS CLE ARI FLA TEX OAK SD PIT

MLB PAYROLLS
1990–2010

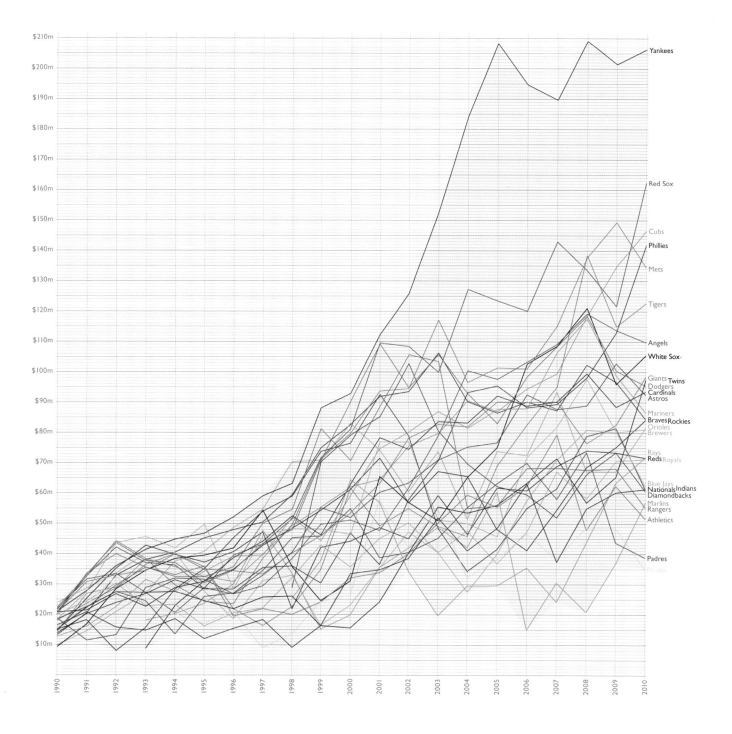

$210m
$200m
$190m
$180m
$170m
$160m
$150m
$140m
$130m
$120m
$110m
$100m
$90m
$80m
$70m
$60m
$50m
$40m
$30m
$20m
$10m

Yankees
Red Sox
Cubs
Phillies
Mets
Tigers
Angels
White Sox
Giants Twins
Dodgers
Cardinals
Astros
Mariners
Braves Rockies
Orioles
Brewers
Rays
Reds Royals
Blue Jays
Nationals Indians
Diamondbacks
Marlins
Rangers
Athletics
Padres
Pirates

1990 1991 1992 1993 1994 1995 1996 1997 1998 1999 2000 2001 2002 2003 2004 2005 2006 2007 2008 2009 2010

DIFFERENCE BETWEEN HIGHEST & LOWEST PAYROLLS IN MLB, NFL, NBA, AND NHL*

MARLINS $36.8M ▶   ◀ YANKEES $201.4M

CHIEFS $83.6M ▶   ◀ RAIDERS $152.4M

HEAT $50.0M ▶   ◀ KNICKS $97.1M

ISLANDERS $33.3M ▶   ◀ RANGERS $66.1M

*MLB 2009, NFL 2008, NBA 2008–09, AND NHL 2008–09 SEASONS

WORLD SERIES WINNERS
HOW THE PLAYERS WERE ACQUIRED, 2000–2010

2000 YANKEES	2001 DIAMONDBACKS	2002 ANGELS	2003 MARLINS	2004 RED SOX	2005 WHITE SOX	2006 CARDINALS	2007 RED SOX	2008 PHILLIES	2009 YANKEES	2010 GIANTS
JETER	BARAJAS	ANDERSON	BECKETT	NIXON	BUEHRLE	DUNCAN	DELCARMEN	BURRELL	CHAMBERLAIN	BUMGARNER
POSADA	KIM	ERSTAD	CABRERA	CABRERA	CREDE	JOHNSON *	ELLSBURY	HAMELS	COKE	CAIN
PETTITTE	BAUTISTA	GLAUS	CASTILLO	EMBREE	ROWAND	MOLINA	LESTER	HOWARD	GARDNER	ISHIKAWA
HERNANDEZ	BROHAWN	LACKEY	GONZALEZ	LOWE	BLUM	PUJOLS	PAPELBON	MADSON	HUGHES	LINCECUM
RIVERA	GONZALEZ	PALMEIRO	REDMOND	MARTINEZ	CONTRERAS	REYES	PEDROIA	MYERS	JETER	POSEY
WILLIAMS	LOPEZ	PERCIVAL	CONINE	MIENTKIEWICZ	COTTS	THOMPSON	YOUKILIS	ROLLINS	POSADA	ROMO
BROSIUS	SCHILLING	SALMON	ENCARNACION	MIRABELLI	EVERETT	BELLIARD	BECKETT	UTLEY	ROBERTSON	J. SANCHEZ
CLEMENS	WILLIAMS	SCHOENEWEIS	LEE	SCHILLING	GARCIA	EDMONDS	CORA	RUIZ	CABRERA	SCHIERHOLTZ
CONE	WOMACK	SHIELDS	LOOPER	VARITEK	GARLAND	MILES	CRISP	BLANTON	CANO	WILSON
HILL	BATISTA	WASHBURN	LOWELL	DAMON	HARRIS	RODRIGUEZ	GAGNE	BRUNTLETT	RIVERA	SANDOVAL
JUSTICE	BELL	B. MOLINA	PAVANO	FOULKE	KONERKO	ROLEN	HINKSE	EYRE	HAIRSTON	FONTENOT
KNOBLAUCH	COLBRUNN	ORTIZ	PENNY	KAPLER	PEREZ	WAINWRIGHT	LOPEZ	LIDGE	HINSKE	LOPEZ
NEAGLE	COUNSELL	RODRIGUEZ	PIERRE	MUELLER	PODSEDNIK	WEAVER	LOWELL	MOYER	MARTE	RAMIREZ
NELSON	CUMMINGS	APPIER	REDMAN	ORTIZ	URIBE	CARPENTER	SCHILLING	STAIRS	MOLINA	F. SANCHEZ
SOJO	FINLEY	FIGGINS	URBINA	RAMIREZ	VIZCAINO	ECKSTEIN	VARITEK	COSTE	RODRIGUEZ	AFFELDT
VIZCAINO	GRACE	FULLMER	WILLIS	REESE	DYE	ENCARNACION	DREW	DURBIN	SWISHER	BURRELL
BELLINGER	JOHNSON	KENNEDY	FOX	TIMLIN	HERMANSON	FLORES	KIELTY	FELIZ	ACEVES	CASILLA
MARTINEZ	MORGAN	OCHOA	HELLING	WAKEFIELD	HERNANDEZ	LOOPER	LUGO	JENKINS	BRUNEY	HUFF
O'NEILL	SANDERS	DONNELLY	HOLLANDSWORTH	ARROYO	IGUCHI	SPIEZIO	OKAJIMA	ROMERO	BURNETT	MOTA
POLONIA	SWINDELL	GIL	RODRIGUEZ	MILLAR	PIERZYNSKI	SUPPAN	ORTIZ	WERTH	DAMON	RENTERIA
STANTON	WITT	J. MOLINA		BELLHORN	POLITTE	TAGUCHI	RAMIREZ	DOBBS	MATSUI	ROWAND
CANSECO	DURAZO	SPIEZIO			WIDGER	WILSON	TIMLIN	VICTORINO	PETTITTE	TORRES
	ANDERSON	WOOTEN			JENKS	KINNEY	MATSUZAKA		SABATHIA	URIBE
	DELLUCCI	ECKSTEIN							TEIXEIRA	ROSS
	MILLER	WEBER								

Only included players who played during that year's World Series.
Original acquisitions listed (i.e., if a player re-signed as a free agent after being traded, he is listed as traded).

* Tyler Johnson, pitcher with the 2006 Cardinals, was drafted by St. Louis in the 2000 amateur draft. He was subsequently drafted by the Athletics in the 2004 rule 5 draft, but returned to the Cardinals in March 2005.

Legend:
- AMATEUR DRAFT
- AMATEUR FREE AGENT
- TRADED
- FREE AGENT
- SELECTED OFF WAIVERS
- RULE 5 DRAFT
- PURCHASED
- CONDITIONAL DEAL
- EXPANSION DRAFT

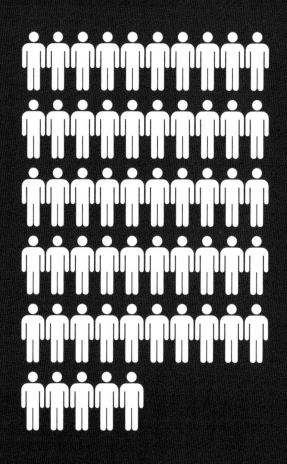

OF THE 106 WORLD SERIES UP TO AND INC. 2010:
51 OF THEM HAVE BEEN CLINCHED AT HOME
55 CLINCHED ON THE ROAD

36 WORLD SERIES HAVE GONE SEVEN GAMES:[1]
18 WON AT HOME, 18 ON THE ROAD

17 WORLD SERIES HAVE BEEN PLAYED IN THE SAME CITY:[2]
6 WON AT HOME, 11 ON THE ROAD

[1] NONE OF THE BEST-OF-NINE SERIES EVER WENT TO A GAME NINE
[2] OBVIOUSLY SAN FRANCISCO AND OAKLAND ARE SEPARATE CITIES,
BUT THEY'RE CLOSE ENOUGH TO BE INCLUDED HERE

OFF DAYS

REGULAR SEASON VS. POSTSEASON: THE 2008 PHILLIES AND RAYS

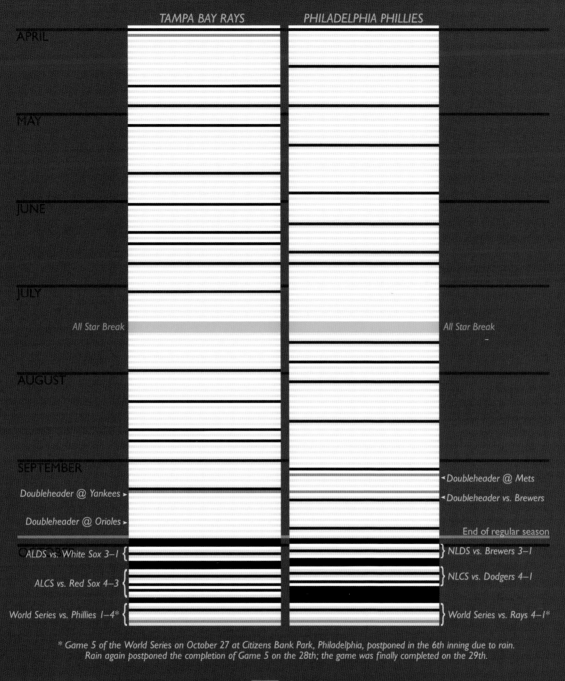

TAMPA BAY RAYS   PHILADELPHIA PHILLIES

APRIL

MAY

JUNE

JULY

All Star Break   *All Star Break*

AUGUST

SEPTEMBER

◄ *Doubleheader @ Mets*
◄ *Doubleheader vs. Brewers*

Doubleheader @ Yankees ►

Doubleheader @ Orioles ►

End of regular season

ALDS vs. White Sox 3–1 {   } NLDS vs. Brewers 3–1

ALCS vs. Red Sox 4–3 {   } NLCS vs. Dodgers 4–1

World Series vs. Phillies 1–4* {   } World Series vs. Rays 4–1*

** Game 5 of the World Series on October 27 at Citizens Bank Park, Philadelphia, postponed in the 6th inning due to rain.
Rain again postponed the completion of Game 5 on the 28th; the game was finally completed on the 29th.*

- Game
- Off day
- Postponed game

LONGEST CHAMPIONSHIP DROUGHTS
YOU GOTTA FEEL FOR THOSE LONG-SUFFERING MARLINS FANS, HUH?

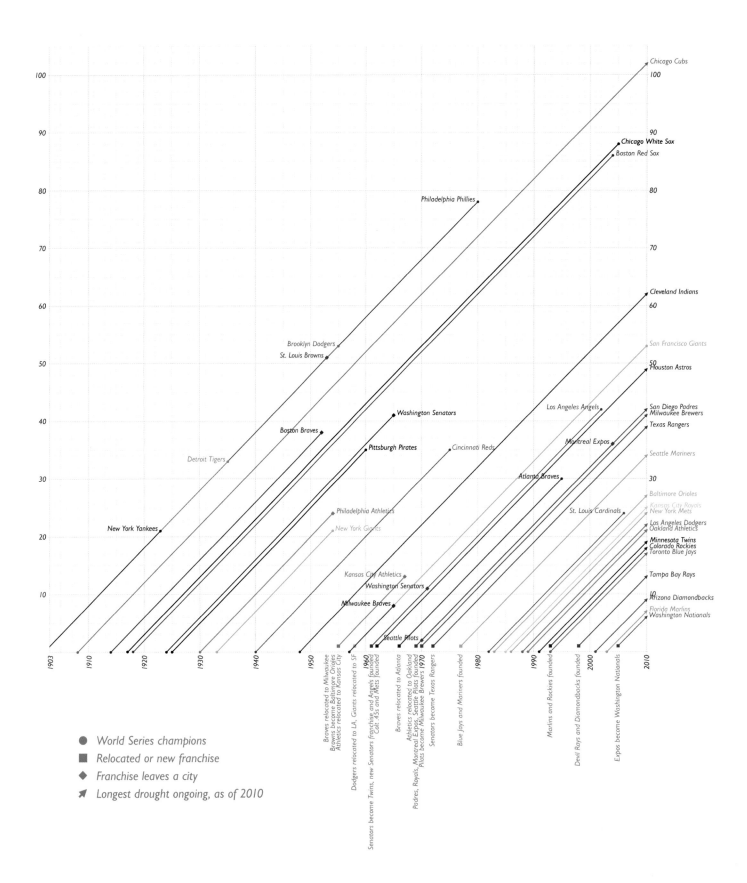

● World Series champions
■ Relocated or new franchise
◆ Franchise leaves a city
✈ Longest drought ongoing, as of 2010

Masochistic Mets Fan During the 2009 World Series

PEDRO (DRAWN WHILE DRUNK, WATCHING GAME 6 OF THE 2009 WORLD SERIES AT AROUND 3:00 A.M., CENTRAL EUROPEAN TIME)

THE 2009 YANKEES AND METS
ON THE BACK PAGE OF THE *NEW YORK POST*
DURING THE BASEBALL REGULAR SEASON

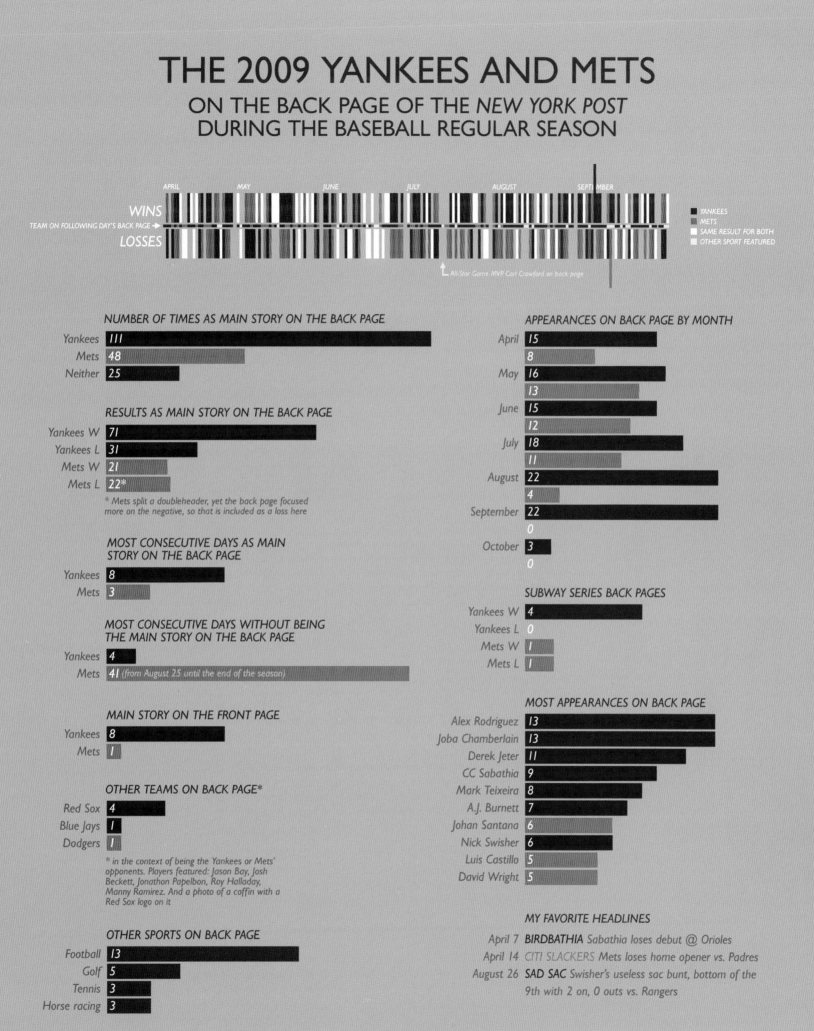

APRIL   MAY   JUNE   JULY   AUGUST   SEPTEMBER

WINS

TEAM ON FOLLOWING DAY'S BACK PAGE →

LOSSES

- YANKEES
- METS
- SAME RESULT FOR BOTH
- OTHER SPORT FEATURED

↑ *All-Star Game MVP Carl Crawford on back page*

NUMBER OF TIMES AS MAIN STORY ON THE BACK PAGE

- Yankees 111
- Mets 48
- Neither 25

RESULTS AS MAIN STORY ON THE BACK PAGE

- Yankees W 71
- Yankees L 31
- Mets W 21
- Mets L 22*

* Mets split a doubleheader, yet the back page focused more on the negative, so that is included as a loss here

MOST CONSECUTIVE DAYS AS MAIN STORY ON THE BACK PAGE

- Yankees 8
- Mets 3

MOST CONSECUTIVE DAYS WITHOUT BEING THE MAIN STORY ON THE BACK PAGE

- Yankees 4
- Mets 41 *(from August 25 until the end of the season)*

MAIN STORY ON THE FRONT PAGE

- Yankees 8
- Mets 1

OTHER TEAMS ON BACK PAGE*

- Red Sox 4
- Blue Jays 1
- Dodgers 1

* in the context of being the Yankees or Mets' opponents. Players featured: Jason Bay, Josh Beckett, Jonathon Papelbon, Roy Halladay, Manny Ramirez. And a photo of a coffin with a Red Sox logo on it

OTHER SPORTS ON BACK PAGE

- Football 13
- Golf 5
- Tennis 3
- Horse racing 3

APPEARANCES ON BACK PAGE BY MONTH

- April 15 / 8
- May 16 / 13
- June 15 / 12
- July 18 / 11
- August 22 / 4
- September 22 / 0
- October 3 / 0

SUBWAY SERIES BACK PAGES

- Yankees W 4
- Yankees L 0
- Mets W 1
- Mets L 1

MOST APPEARANCES ON BACK PAGE

- Alex Rodriguez 13
- Joba Chamberlain 13
- Derek Jeter 11
- CC Sabathia 9
- Mark Teixeira 8
- A.J. Burnett 7
- Johan Santana 6
- Nick Swisher 6
- Luis Castillo 5
- David Wright 5

MY FAVORITE HEADLINES

April 7 **BIRDBATHIA** *Sabathia loses debut @ Orioles*

April 14 CITI SLACKERS *Mets loses home opener vs. Padres*

August 26 **SAD SAC** *Swisher's useless sac bunt, bottom of the 9th with 2 on, 0 outs vs. Rangers*

Since 1903, the Boston Red Sox have played 2,049 games against the New York Highlanders/Yankees, and won 925 of them. If a Red Sox fan, like the popular T-shirt says, also supports whoever beats the New York Yankees, he would have supported another team for a total of 8,646 games (from the start of the 1903 season up to and including the 2010 season). Sadly for the whoever-beats-New-York fan, only two teams have a winning record against the Yankees: the Los Angeles Dodgers (who've won 15, lost 13) and the Washington Nationals (who've won 4, lost 2), but no *franchise* has a winning record against the Yankees in regular- and post-season games, including the Brooklyn/L.A. Dodgers and Expos/Nationals. Here's a chart showing who has beaten the Yankees the most.

1915–18 BOSTON RED SOX
THREE WORLD SERIES AND ONE WORLD WAR

| 1906 | 1907 | 1908 | 1909 | 1910 | 1911 | 1912 | 1913 | 1914 | 1915 | 1916 | 1917 | 1918 | 1919 | 1920 | 1921 | 1922 |

BILL CARRIGAN (PLAYER/MGR)
JACK BARRY (PLAYER/MGR)
ED BARROW (MGR)

PINCH THOMAS
DICK HOBLITZELL
HEINIE WAGNER
EVERETT SCOTT
LARRY GARDNER
TRIS SPEAKER
DUFFY LEWIS
HARRY HOOPER
HAL JANVRIN
JACK BARRY
DEL GAINER
HICK CADY
BILL CARRIGAN
OLAF HENRIKSEN
MIKE MCNALLY
CHICK SHORTEN
BILL RODGERS
RICHARD HALEY
WALLY REHG
TILLIE WALKER
SAM AGNEW
JIMMY WALSH
JIMMY COONEY
WALLY MAYER
STUFFY MCINNIS
DAVE SHEAN
FRED THOMAS
GEORGE WHITEMAN
AMOS STRUNK
WALLY SCHANG
GEORGE COCHRAN
JACK STANSBURY
JACK COFFEY
FRANK TRUESDALE
WALTER BARBARE
HACK MILLER
EUSEBIO GONZALEZ
RED BLUHM

RUBE FOSTER
ERNIE SHORE
BABE RUTH
DUTCH LEONARD
SMOKY JOE WOOD
CARL MAYS
RAY COLLINS
VEAN GREGG
HERB PENNOCK
RALPH CONSTOCK
GUY COOPER
SAD SAM JONES
WELDON WYCKOFF
MARTY MCHALE
KING BADER
BULLET JOE BUSH
WALT KINNEY
VINCE MOLYNEAUX
JEAN DUBUC
DICK MCCABE
BILL PERTICA

RED SOX WORLD SERIES WINNING TEAMS
RED SOX
PART OF SEASON SPENT WITH RED SOX
OTHER TEAMS
MILITARY SERVICE OF RED SOX PLAYERS

1975–76 CINCINNATI REDS
BIG, RED, AND SOMEWHAT MACHINE-LIKE

1963 1964 1965 1966 1967 1968 1969 1970 1971 1972 1973 1974 1975 1976 1977 1978 1979 1980 1981 1982 1983 1984 1985 1986 1987 1988

BOB HOWSAM (GM)
SPARKY ANDERSON (MGR)

JOHNNY BENCH
TONY PEREZ
JOE MORGAN
DAVE CONCEPCION
PETE ROSE
GEORGE FOSTER
CESAR GERONIMO
KEN GRIFFEY
BILL PLUMMER
DAN DRIESSEN
ED ARMBRISTER
DON WERNER
DOUG FLYNN
DARRYL CHANEY
MERV RETTENMUND
TERRY CROWLEY
JOHN VUKOVICH
MIKE LUM
BOB BAILEY
JOEL YOUNGBLOOD

GARY NOLAN
JACK BILLINGHAM
FRED NORMAN
DON GULLETT
PAT DARCY
WILL McENANEY
PEDRO BORBON
RAWLY EASTWICK
CLAY CARROLL
TOM CARROLL
CLAY KIRBY
TOM HALL
PAT ZACHRY
SANTO ALCALA
MANNY SARMIENTO
RICH HINTON
JOE HENDERSON

REDS WORLD SERIES WINNING TEAM
REDS
PART OF SEASON SPENT WITH REDS
OTHER TEAMS

1986 NEW YORK METS
ASSEMBLING & DISMANTLING THE WORLD SERIES WINNING TEAM

METS WORLD SERIES WINNING TEAM
METS
PART OF SEASON SPENT WITH METS
OTHER TEAMS

1997 & 2003 FLORIDA MARLINS
CHAMPIONS, FIRE SALE, CHAMPIONS

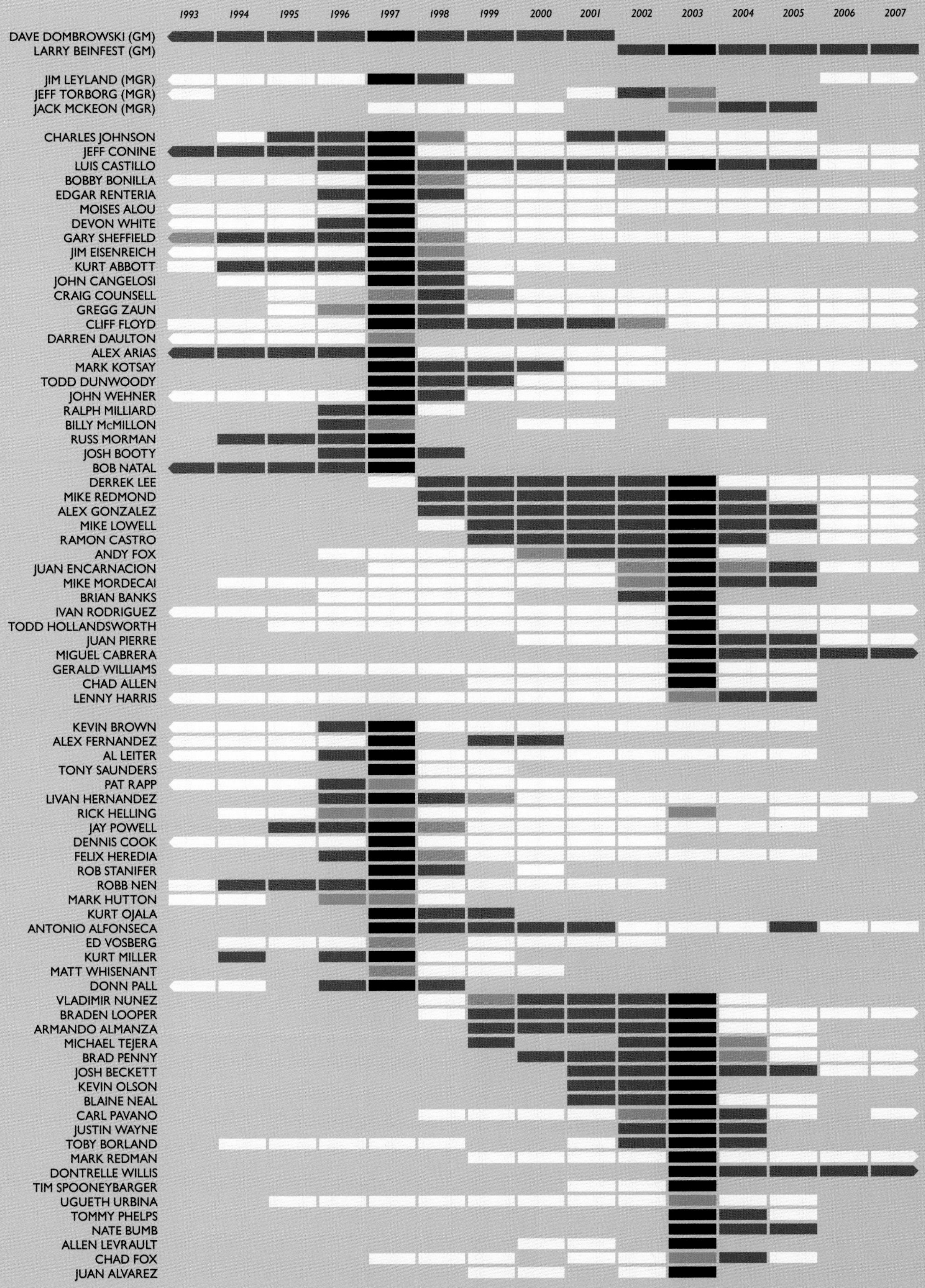

	1993	1994	1995	1996	1997	1998	1999	2000	2001	2002	2003	2004	2005	2006	2007

DAVE DOMBROWSKI (GM)
LARRY BEINFEST (GM)

JIM LEYLAND (MGR)
JEFF TORBORG (MGR)
JACK MCKEON (MGR)

CHARLES JOHNSON
JEFF CONINE
LUIS CASTILLO
BOBBY BONILLA
EDGAR RENTERIA
MOISES ALOU
DEVON WHITE
GARY SHEFFIELD
JIM EISENREICH
KURT ABBOTT
JOHN CANGELOSI
CRAIG COUNSELL
GREGG ZAUN
CLIFF FLOYD
DARREN DAULTON
ALEX ARIAS
MARK KOTSAY
TODD DUNWOODY
JOHN WEHNER
RALPH MILLIARD
BILLY McMILLON
RUSS MORMAN
JOSH BOOTY
BOB NATAL
DERREK LEE
MIKE REDMOND
ALEX GONZALEZ
MIKE LOWELL
RAMON CASTRO
ANDY FOX
JUAN ENCARNACION
MIKE MORDECAI
BRIAN BANKS
IVAN RODRIGUEZ
TODD HOLLANDSWORTH
JUAN PIERRE
MIGUEL CABRERA
GERALD WILLIAMS
CHAD ALLEN
LENNY HARRIS

KEVIN BROWN
ALEX FERNANDEZ
AL LEITER
TONY SAUNDERS
PAT RAPP
LIVAN HERNANDEZ
RICK HELLING
JAY POWELL
DENNIS COOK
FELIX HEREDIA
ROB STANIFER
ROBB NEN
MARK HUTTON
KURT OJALA
ANTONIO ALFONSECA
ED VOSBERG
KURT MILLER
MATT WHISENANT
DONN PALL
VLADIMIR NUNEZ
BRADEN LOOPER
ARMANDO ALMANZA
MICHAEL TEJERA
BRAD PENNY
JOSH BECKETT
KEVIN OLSON
BLAINE NEAL
CARL PAVANO
JUSTIN WAYNE
TOBY BORLAND
MARK REDMAN
DONTRELLE WILLIS
TIM SPOONEYBARGER
UGUETH URBINA
TOMMY PHELPS
NATE BUMB
ALLEN LEVRAULT
CHAD FOX
JUAN ALVAREZ

1998–2002 FLORIDA MARLINS
THE PLAYERS WHO MISSED OUT

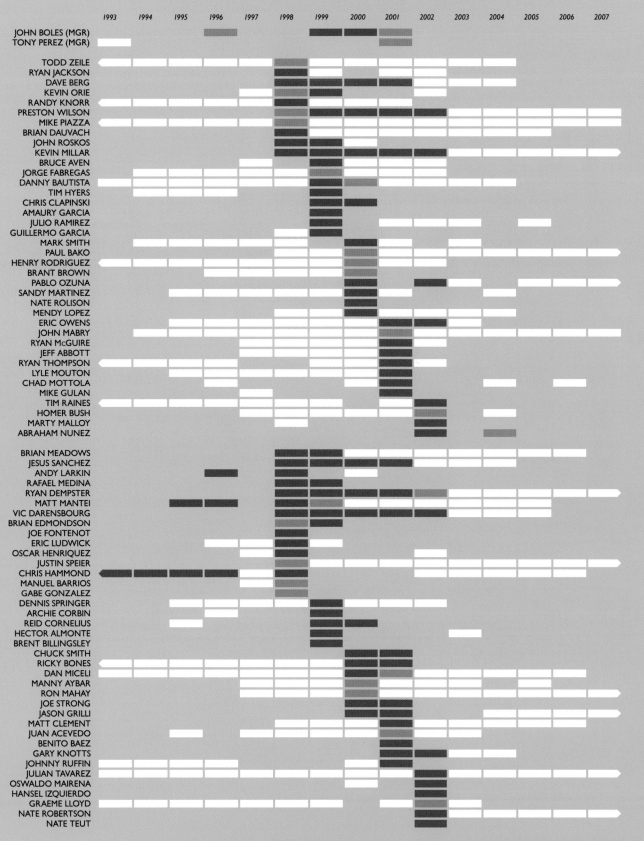

INTERLEAGUE PLAY

NUMBER OF TEAMS WITH WINNING INTERLEAGUE RECORDS PER SEASON

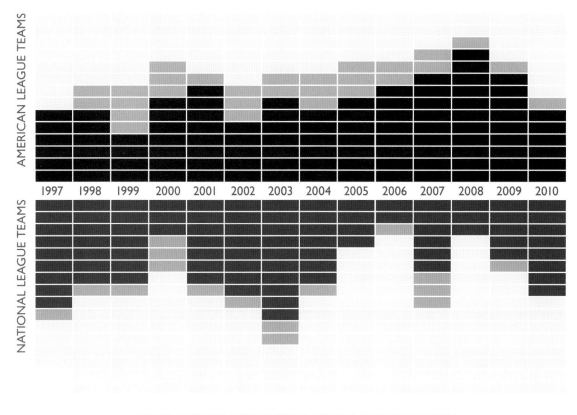

AMERICAN LEAGUE TEAMS

1997 1998 1999 2000 2001 2002 2003 2004 2005 2006 2007 2008 2009 2010

NATIONAL LEAGUE TEAMS

WHICH LEAGUE WON INTERLEAGUE PLAY EACH SEASON?

WHICH LEAGUE WON THE ALL-STAR GAME EACH SEASON?
TIE

WHICH LEAGUE'S REPRESENTATIVE WON THE WORLD SERIES EACH SEASON?

EACH TEAM'S INTERLEAGUE RECORD

YANKEES	METS
ANGELS	GIANTS
RED SOX	CARDINALS
WHITE SOX	MARLINS
ATHLETICS	BRAVES
TWINS	BREWERS*
TIGERS	DODGERS
MARINERS	ROCKIES
RANGERS	CUBS
INDIANS	PHILLIES
(DEVIL) RAYS	ASTROS
ORIOLES	REDS
ROYALS	EXPOS/NATIONALS
BLUE JAYS	DIAMONDBACKS
	PADRES
	PIRATES

WINNING INTERLEAGUE SEASON RECORD   .500 INTERLEAGUE SEASON RECORD
* BREWERS IN AMERICAN LEAGUE FOR 1997 SEASON

DEFENSIVE POSITIONING
TWINS AT BLUE JAYS, JULY 6, 2010

BLUE JAYS DEFENSE

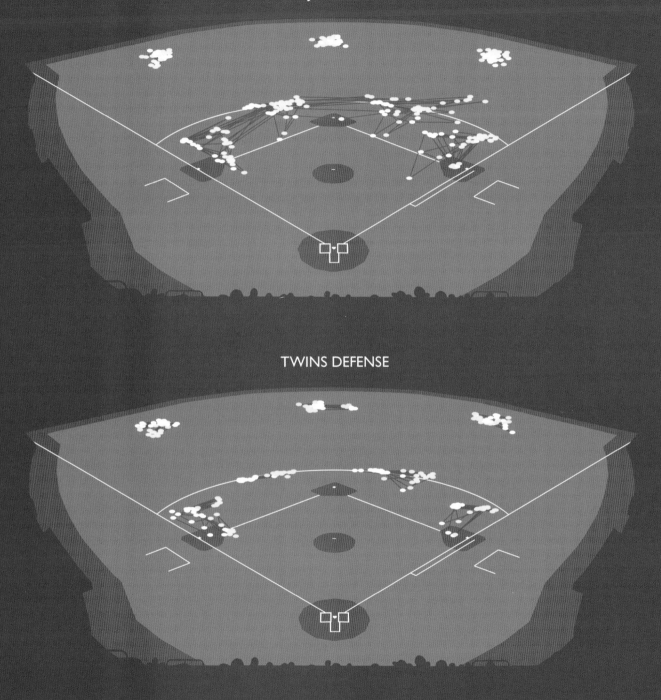

TWINS DEFENSE

I sat in Section 524 Row 22 Seat 11, the seat at the top of the stadium, dead center, and took a photograph of every at-bat during the first pitch. Obviously, it was difficult to get a photograph at the exact same point, but every photograph was taken during the pitch. The above graphics are plotting where the defense stood for each at-bat.

WHITE = Right-handed batter YELLOW = Left-handed batter

NOLAN RYAN
A MAJOR LEAGUE RECORD 27 SEASONS

FIRST MAJOR LEAGUE GAME: SEPTEMBER 11, 1966, FOR THE NEW YORK METS
LAST MAJOR LEAGUE GAME: SEPTEMBER 22, 1993, FOR THE TEXAS RANGERS

Number One on the
Billboard Hot 100
when Ryan first pitched
in the majors:

"YOU CAN'T HURRY LOVE"
THE SUPREMES

Number One on the
Billboard Hot 100
when Ryan last pitched
in the majors:

"DREAMLOVER"
MARIAH CAREY

NOLAN RYAN
OR TWO 8–7 PITCHERS?

NOLAN RYAN WENT 16–14 FOR THE CALIFORNIA ANGELS IN 1979. ANGELS OWNER BUZZIE BAVASI DECLINED TO RE-SIGN RYAN AFTER HIS CONTRACT EXPIRED AT THE END OF THE SEASON, SAYING THAT ALL HE NEEDED TO COME UP WITH WAS TWO 8–7 PITCHERS.

IN THE 1979 SEASON, THREE PITCHERS HAD 8–7 RECORDS: JOE SAMBITO (HOUSTON ASTROS), ELIAS SOSA (MONTREAL EXPOS), AND BRIAN KINGMAN (OAKLAND ATHLETICS).

SO, HOW DOES ANY COMBINATION OF TWO OF THE THREE COMPARE WITH NOLAN RYAN?

	INNINGS PITCHED	STRIKEOUTS	ERA
NOLAN	222.2	223	3.60
JS & ES	188.0	142	1.87
JS & BK	204.0	141	3.18
ES & BK	209.1	117	3.22

	HITS	WALKS	WHIP
NOLAN	169	114	1.271
JS & ES	157	60	1.154
JS & BK	193	56	1.221
ES & BK	190	70	1.242

	RUNS / EARNED RUNS	HOME RUNS
NOLAN	104/89	15
JS & ES	44/39	10
JS & BK	79/72	18
ES & BK	83/75	12

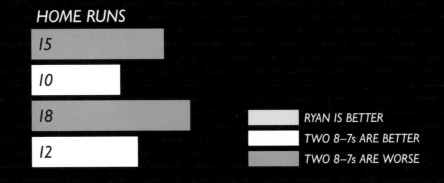

RYAN IS BETTER
TWO 8–7s ARE BETTER
TWO 8–7s ARE WORSE

ROGER CLEMENS

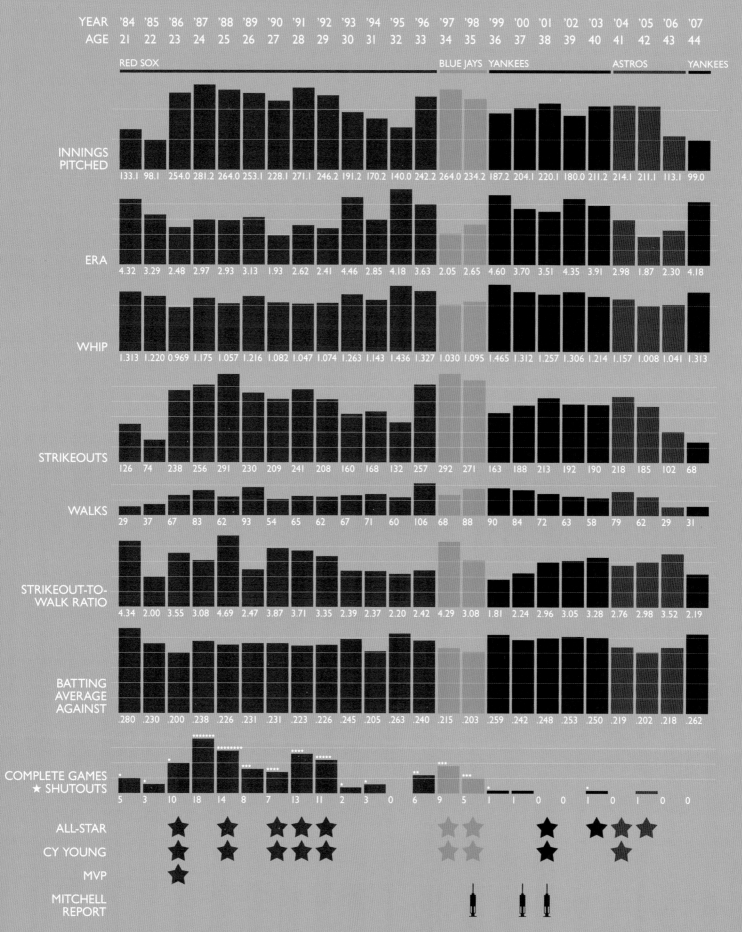

YEAR	'84	'85	'86	'87	'88	'89	'90	'91	'92	'93	'94	'95	'96	'97	'98	'99	'00	'01	'02	'03	'04	'05	'06	'07
AGE	21	22	23	24	25	26	27	28	29	30	31	32	33	34	35	36	37	38	39	40	41	42	43	44

RED SOX · BLUE JAYS · YANKEES · ASTROS · YANKEES

INNINGS PITCHED
133.1 · 98.1 · 254.0 · 281.2 · 264.0 · 253.1 · 228.1 · 271.1 · 246.2 · 191.2 · 170.2 · 140.0 · 242.2 · 264.0 · 234.2 · 187.2 · 204.1 · 220.1 · 180.0 · 211.2 · 214.1 · 211.1 · 113.1 · 99.0

ERA
4.32 · 3.29 · 2.48 · 2.97 · 2.93 · 3.13 · 1.93 · 2.62 · 2.41 · 4.46 · 2.85 · 4.18 · 3.63 · 2.05 · 2.65 · 4.60 · 3.70 · 3.51 · 4.35 · 3.91 · 2.98 · 1.87 · 2.30 · 4.18

WHIP
1.313 · 1.220 · 0.969 · 1.175 · 1.057 · 1.216 · 1.082 · 1.047 · 1.074 · 1.263 · 1.143 · 1.436 · 1.327 · 1.030 · 1.095 · 1.465 · 1.312 · 1.257 · 1.306 · 1.214 · 1.157 · 1.008 · 1.041 · 1.313

STRIKEOUTS
126 · 74 · 238 · 256 · 291 · 230 · 209 · 241 · 208 · 160 · 168 · 132 · 257 · 292 · 271 · 163 · 188 · 213 · 192 · 190 · 218 · 185 · 102 · 68

WALKS
29 · 37 · 67 · 83 · 62 · 93 · 54 · 65 · 62 · 67 · 71 · 60 · 106 · 68 · 88 · 90 · 84 · 72 · 63 · 58 · 79 · 62 · 29 · 31

STRIKEOUT-TO-WALK RATIO
4.34 · 2.00 · 3.55 · 3.08 · 4.69 · 2.47 · 3.87 · 3.71 · 3.35 · 2.39 · 2.37 · 2.20 · 2.42 · 4.29 · 3.08 · 1.81 · 2.24 · 2.96 · 3.05 · 3.28 · 2.76 · 2.98 · 3.52 · 2.19

BATTING AVERAGE AGAINST
.280 · .230 · .200 · .238 · .226 · .231 · .231 · .223 · .226 · .245 · .205 · .263 · .240 · .215 · .203 · .259 · .242 · .248 · .253 · .250 · .219 · .202 · .218 · .262

COMPLETE GAMES ★ SHUTOUTS
5 · 3 · 10 · 18 · 14 · 8 · 7 · 13 · 11 · 2 · 3 · 0 · 6 · 9 · 5 · 1 · 1 · 0 · 0 · 1 · 0 · 1 · 0 · 0

ALL-STAR

CY YOUNG

MVP

MITCHELL REPORT

JOHN 3:16
For God so loved the world that he gave his only son a wicked slider, so that everyone who believes in his stuff might not get fired by the owner.

PITCHERS WITH 3–16 SINGLE SEASON RECORDS
Rick Honeycutt (1987, Los Angeles Dodgers/Oakland Athletics), Frank Sullivan (1961, Philadelphia Phillies), Lou Knerr (1946, Philadelpia Athletics), and the wonderfully named Burleigh Grimes (1917, Pittsburgh Pirates).

WELCOME TO BRADENIA
AN AUTONOMOUS REGION OF OAKLAND ATHLETICA

OAKLAND
ATHLETICA

BRADENIA

MONARCH: KING DALLAS I
POPULATION: I
VISA REQUIREMENTS: NOT BEING A-ROD

FIRSTBASELAND WAS BRIEFLY ANNEXED IN 2010
WITH ALL VISA REQUIREMENTS FROM TAMPA BAY BEING REJECTED

"CULA A-ROD"

ALEX RODRIGUEZ'S SALARY
A VERY TALL STACK OF PENNIES

A-Rod's 2010 salary and prorated bonus of $33,000,000
equal a 3,178.3-mile-high stack of pennies

CENTAURS IN BASEBALL
WHY THEY WOULDN'T MAKE GOOD THIRD BASEMEN

1. He'd be useless defensively. You gotta imagine he'd have truly awful UZR numbers, like -100 in a season or something. He'd be really easy to bunt on: anything necessitating a dive to his left or right would get past him.

2. Rule 6.03 of the Official Baseball Rules states that "the batter's legal position shall be with both feet within the batter's box." An amendment to the rules might be needed were a centaur to play in the majors. Would "both" mean all of the batter's feet? Or would it mean "both of the batter's front feet"?

3. If a centaur got on base, he'd not be able to take much of a lead or he'd be easily picked off.

4. If he did try to steal a base and slid into the bag, he'd possibly break a leg and have to be shot.

5. Entering and leaving the dugout could be a bit tricky, and his participation in a bench-clearing brawl could end up looking like the aftermath of a G8 riot.

Still, it's quite fun to imagine a tie game, bottom of the 9th, one out, centaur on third, sac fly to right field: how would a catcher block the plate with a centaur bearing down on him?

CC Sabathia

MIKE MORGAN AND MATT STAIRS
DON'T GET TOO COMFORTABLE, FELLAS…

MIKE MORGAN
12 ORGANIZATIONS, 22 TEAMS

OAKLAND ATHLETICS 1978–79	
VANCOUVER CANADIANS 1978	AAA
OGDEN A'S 1979–80	AAA
NEW YORK YANKEES 1982	
NASHVILLE SOUNDS 1981	AA
TORONTO BLUE JAYS 1983	
SYRACUSE CHIEFS 1983–84	AAA
SEATTLE MARINERS 1985–87	
CALGARY CANNONS 1985	AAA
BALTIMORE ORIOLES 1988	
ROCHESTER RED WINGS 1988	AAA
LOS ANGELES DODGERS 1989–91	
CHICAGO CUBS 1992–95, 1998	
ORLANDO CUBS 1995	AA
ST. LOUIS CARDINALS 1995–96	
LOUISVILLE REDBIRDS 1996	AAA
ST. PETERSBURG CARDINALS 1996	A+
CINCINNATI REDS 1996–97	
MINNESOTA TWINS 1998	
TEXAS RANGERS 1999	
ARIZONA DIAMONDBACKS 2000–2	
TUCSON SIDEWINDERS 2001, 2002	AAA

MATT STAIRS
13 ORGANIZATIONS, 24 TEAMS*

MONTREAL EXPOS 1992–93	
INDIANAPOLIS INDIANS 1992	AAA
OTTAWA LYNX 1993	AAA
JACKSONVILLE EXPOS 1990	AA
HARRISBURG SENATORS 1991	AA
WEST PALM BEACH EXPOS 1989–90	A+
ROCKFROM EXPOS 1989	A
JAMESTOWN EXPOS 1989	A-
CHUNICHI DRAGONS 1993	NPB
BOSTON RED SOX 1995	
PAWTUCKET RED SOX 1995	AAA
NEW BRITAIN RED SOX 1994	AA
OAKLAND ATHLETICS 1996–2000	
EDMONTON TRAPPERS 1996	AAA
CHICAGO CUBS 2001	
MILWAUKEE BREWERS 2002	
PITTSBURGH PIRATES 2003	
NASHVILLE SOUNDS 2003	AAA
KANSAS CITY ROYALS 2004–6	
TEXAS RANGERS 2006	
DETROIT TIGERS 2006	
TORONTO BLUE JAYS 2007–8	
PHILADELPHIA PHILLIES 2008–9	
SAN DIEGO PADRES 2010	

* STILL ACTIVE, SO YOU NEVER KNOW

BENGIE, JOSÉ, & YADIER
THE WONDERFUL WORLD OF THE MOLINA BROTHERS

BENGIE — **JOSÉ** — **YADIER**

	BENGIE	JOSÉ	YADIER
	Catcher	Catcher	Catcher
	Bats: right Throws: right	Bats: right Throws: right	Bats: right Throws: right
	Born July 20, 1974	Born June 3, 1975	Born July 13, 1982
	Signed by Angels, 1993	Drafted by Cubs, 1993	Drafted by Cardinals, 2000

Year	Bengie	José	Yadier	Year
1998	Angels			1998
1999	Angels	Cubs		1999
2000	Angels			2000
2001	Angels	Angels		2001
2002	Angels (won World Series ring)	Angels (won World Series ring)		2002
2003	Angels	Angels		2003
2004	Angels	Angels	Cardinals	2004
2005	Angels	Angels	Cardinals	2005
2006	Blue Jays	Angels	Cardinals (won World Series ring)	2006
2007	Giants	Angels / Yankees	Cardinals	2007
2008	Giants	Yankees	Cardinals	2008
2009	Giants	Yankees (won World Series ring)	Cardinals	2009
2010	Giants / Rangers (won World Series ring)	Blue Jays	Cardinals	2010

DID YOU KNOW?

Outside of baseball, the Molinas share lots of hobbies and skills.
They include: gardening, playing marbles, picking berries, starting campfires, toasting marshmallows, teaching toddlers to walk, doing frog impressions, trying to attract timid stray cats with saucers of milk, changing tires, fighting midgets with honor, gold panning, taking a dump in the woods, burning bugs with magnifying glasses, clam digging, and riding clown bicycles.

And if you ever need three people to help you move into a new apartment, the Molinas will always lift boxes correctly.

.405701754
TED WILLIAMS' 1941 BATTING AVERAGE, DAY BY DAY

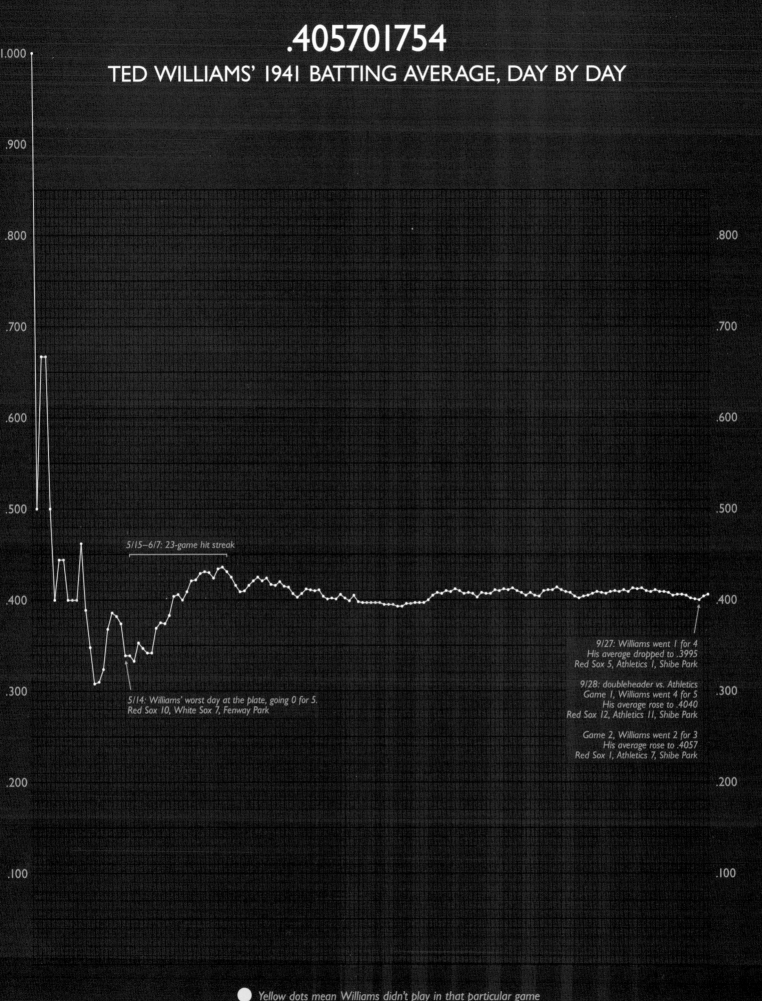

5/15–6/7: 23-game hit streak

5/14: Williams' worst day at the plate, going 0 for 5.
Red Sox 10, White Sox 7, Fenway Park

9/27: Williams went 1 for 4
His average dropped to .3995
Red Sox 5, Athletics 1, Shibe Park

9/28: doubleheader vs. Athletics
Game 1, Williams went 4 for 5
His average rose to .4040
Red Sox 12, Athletics 11, Shibe Park

Game 2, Williams went 2 for 3
His average rose to .4057
Red Sox 1, Athletics 7, Shibe Park

Yellow dots mean Williams didn't play in that particular game

CR 25 MARCH 2010

Kevin Youkalyptus

RANDY AND THE DOVE
THE DOVE SPEAKS FOR THE FIRST TIME

We caught up with Jake, the dove who was killed by a Randy Johnson pitch during an Arizona Diamondbacks spring training game on March 24, 2001. He now lives in Heaven. This is his story.

Well, funnily enough it was the first spring training game I'd been to. My wife and I live in Phoenix, and we had a spare few days, so we decided to fly down to Tucson to see the Diamondbacks–Giants game. I'm from Phoenix—big D-backs fan—and my wife, Dana, is originally from the Bay Area. We met there, actually; I was there on vacation, just flying around Golden Gate Park, and there was this woman giving away seeds near the tennis courts. Dana and I started talking, and the rest is history. Anyway, her team's the Giants. So we flew down to Tucson Electric Park to see the game. Lovely bright sunny afternoon— perfect baseball weather.

I was enjoying the game, and the D-backs were winning. I was super-excited to see Randy Johnson; he was my favorite pitcher. Three-time Cy Young winner, six-time All Star at the time: you can't argue with that, can you? I was teasing Dana, saying that this season we'd win the division again like '99. She was saying that it didn't matter that the Giants were losing, it was only spring training. Soon after the seventh-inning stretch, we were getting a little hungry, and she spotted a kid over behind the first-base dugout who'd dropped his hot dog. I don't understand why you humans don't like eating food that's been on the floor, but we're not complaining: all the more for us! So we decided to get in there to get that hot dog bun before any other doves or pigeons got in there.

To be honest, I don't remember much after that. I know I was flying lower than Dana; in front of her, too. And I remember thinking how tall Randy Johnson looked close up. After that, it's all a blank. I've seen it on TV since then, and you can tell I'm not flying as I normally would. I look a little tired; maybe that's why I was flying so low. The wife and I had had a late one the night before, if you know what I mean! But, yeah, my head came clean off, huh? Feathers everywhere! Needless to say, I was up here in Heaven fairly promptly. I was sad at first. I really missed Dana. I mean, I'm glad it was me and not her that got beaned, but I missed her a lot. But she's up here with me now, so that's nice. We've got cable up here, so I get to see a fair number of Diamondbacks games. The World Series that year against the Yankees was insane. Absolutely magic. I was a bit disappointed, though, when Randy got traded to the Yankees, but money rules, I guess. Anyway, it's all in the past now. Every now and again someone will bring it up—it's difficult not to see the stitches around my neck—and I think Dana's bored of hearing the story, but she humors me.

By the way, if Dave Winfield is reading this: You better watch your back. There's a seagull up here who is still very, *very* pissed at you!

Mark Fidrych

ICHIRO IS AWESOME

(YOU DIDN'T NEED A CHART TO CONVINCE YOU, DID YOU?)

"ROCK'N ME"
BY THE STEVE MILLER BAND

EVERETT GIANTS

MARINERS

TACOMA

TWINS

SCRANTON/WILKES-BARRE
RED BARONS

INDIANS

YANKEES

CUBS

PHILLIES

PIRATES

ALTOONA CURVE

GIANTS

FRESNO GIANTS

DODGERS

DIAMONDBACKS
PHOENIX FIREBIRDS

TUCSON SIDEWINDERS

BRAVES

SHREVEPORT CAPTAINS

— MILLER'S JOURNEY
● MULHOLLAND'S MLB TEAMS
● MULHOLLAND'S MiLB TEAMS

I'm quite sure you're aware of the Steve Miller Band song "Rock'n Me." If you turn on a classic rock station in your car, the odds of your hearing it before your journey is over are more or less 1:1.

In case you need your memory refreshed, and without quoting the lyrics correctly (thus avoiding having to pay to use them), Mr. Miller went from Phoenix, Az., to Tacoma, then to Philadelphia, Atlanta, and Los Angeles. He ended up in Northern California, where, according to Steve, the girls are warm, which is nice to know. He did all of this so that he could be with his sweet baby. Yeah.

Aside from wondering what sort of relationship he has with his sweet baby if, after all of that traveling to be with her, he feels the need to mention the temperature and/or friendliness of Northern California girls, I wondered if any player has ever played for all of the teams located in those places.

And the answer: almost.

Left-handed pitcher Terry Mulholland came so damn close. He played 5 games for the Diamondbacks, 169 games for the Phillies, 73 games for the Giants (I've assumed San Francisco is where Miller went because it's his hometown), 70 games for the Braves, and 40 games for the Dodgers. He also played 12 games for the Mariners, but not for their AAA affiliate, the Tacoma Rainiers. It is possible, though, that he may have played *against* or *in* Tacoma, as he played 90 games in the Pacific Coast League over six seasons for the Phoenix Firebirds and Tucson Sidewinders.

It's a good job there was no need for a baseball infographic about "The Joker" because I'd have been forced to use a terrible pun: the pompatus of glove.

BEER AND LOATHING IN SEATTLE

Whenever the calendar stumbles toward one of the season's Yankees–Red Sox game, the commentator reminds us that this is the greatest rivalry in sports. Aside from the merits of the claim (surely rivalries like India vs. Pakistan in cricket or Celtic vs. Rangers in Scottish soccer are bigger rivalries), Yankees–Red Sox is one of the few moments in the slick, managed entertainment product of professional sports where something very specific, very crucial, and very real happens: we don't just root root root for our own team, we hate hate hate someone else's team. Most of the time in the media coverage of sports this is overlooked. Hating Manchester United if you're a Liverpool fan, the Steelers if you're a Browns fan, Michigan if you're an Ohio State fan, the Giants if you're a Dodgers fan: it's an integral part of your life as a fan.

It's one of the few areas in my life where I accept politically indefensible irrationality, too. If I'm watching, say, Liverpool play Fulham, and a Fulham defender so much as touches the garment of a Liverpool player, I'm ready to see that defender sent to the Tower of London to be hanged, drawn, and quartered. If that scenario had a Manchester United player cynically mowed down by the Fulham defender, I'd be wanting the Man Utd player sent off for feigning injury and the defender to be knighted by the Queen.

(Before I go on, a quick word for Red Sox fans: the following words are going to be about your team. I'm a fan of the team you hate the most. Thus the feeling is mutual. But I have some good friends who are Red Sox fans; one in particular, we email daily about all kinds of stuff, mostly baseball matters, and we manage to be entirely civil about things. That's a bit more trying when one of our teams is crushing the other, but please don't take this personally. I really like David Ortiz; I watched Youkilis with amazement; and of course, there's no need to convince me how great Ted Williams was. Feel free to take some Wite-Out and substitute all mentions of the Red Sox with the word "Yankees" and vice versa, or Mets–Phillies, or Twins–White Sox, or Cards–Cubs, or Marlins–whoever.)

In May 2009, I was living in Washington state. My friend Claire and I drove to Seattle to see the Mariners play the Red Sox. It was the very first time in my life that I had gone to any sporting event primarily to root against a team. Of course, there was the joy of getting to see Ichiro when in Seattle, but I'd done that a few times already that season. My day was entirely devoted to hating his opponents.

My friend is a Mariners fan, so for once I was entirely on her side of things at an M's game. We arrived in Seattle in midafternoon and had a nice walk around, spotting a few more Red Sox jerseys and caps than one would normally see. We passed a guy in a Red Sox T-shirt. He pointed at my Montreal Expos cap and shouted, "Cool cap!" I pointed at his shirt, smiled, and gave him a thumbs-down. He laughed, we laughed, a funny moment for all. But as the afternoon went on, I began to realize that wearing a red sweatshirt probably wasn't the best idea. I might look like . . . one of them. So to offset potentially being identified as a Sox fan, I went into the Mariners store and bought a replica cap of a 1930s Pacific Coast League team, the Seattle Rainiers. I could now fake being a Mariners fan with at least a whiff of sincerity, even though any rooting I did was entirely the support of a Yankees fan wanting to see Boston lose.

Inside Safeco, there were loads of Red Sox fans. This was the first game I'd been to where the road team was a "big" team, a team with fairly large support across the nation. Boston fans were everywhere. As we walked around, there seemed to be about a 60/40 split in favor of the Mariners, but that was still a heck of a lot of Boston fans. Does that mean 40 percent of metro Seattle inhabit-

ants are closet Red Sox fans? I hope not. They were loud, too. It was horrible. I felt a twisting, a stirring of atavistic emotion inside of me. Every so often I'd see a Sox fan who particularly took my disfancy, and I'd snarl, "Look at that douchebag with the douchey face and douchey cap and that douchebag Pedroia T-shirt."

Claire would then look at me like I was nuts and say, "She's about six years old, Craig!"

There's a pitching speed gun thingy at Safeco. The mannequin dressed up as a batter always wears a Yankees uniform, because the Yankees are universal baseball code for the bad guys. I stood and watched as a couple of men in their late thirties deliberately threw balls at the mannequin's head. (I had a go right after them and, well, with all the energy I could muster, I threw 43 mph. That's not good enough for the majors, is it?)

We sat in the sun in the outfield for a while before the game. I continued chuntering, being a complete dick, really, making the experience less than enjoyable for my friend. Game time approaching, we took our seats in the upper deck. I booed the announcement of the Red Sox lineup, with the biggest boo saved for their catcher. I cheered the Mariners lineup to maintain appearances. But I wasn't really there for them.

The Yankees were three and a half games back of Boston at the time. I kept half an eye on the out-of-town scoreboard, which told me the Yankees were losing 4–2 to the Twins. Things got worse. The Red Sox scored a run in both the first and second, then another two in the third. The Red Sox fans were making all the noise. I grumbled and moaned, not enjoying myself at all. The out-of-town scoreboard showed that New York had got a run, and the bottom of the ninth seemed to be taking ages. Eventually the scoreboard changed to show a final score: Yankees had won 5–4. At that point it became easier to write off a 4–0 Boston lead as one of those things, knowing that my team had won.

Then things changed. Ichiro hit a home run in the fifth. And in the sixth, after another couple of Mariners runs, he hit a second. The Mariners were winning. A loud Red Sox fan in the section in front of ours stood up, looked around, and did his best to shout over the "Let's go Mariners" chants, but found himself a bit more outnumbered than he'd been when his team was winning 4–0. Sean White, Mark Lowe, and David Aardsma came in from the bullpen and gave up only one hit and two walks between them. Ball game over. Mariners win. And, much more important to me, Boston lost.

Why did my innocent, naïve, nonthreateningly English Yankee fandom turn sick and twisted? From where in my heart did such bile spring? Was it just because I saw that New York–Boston was a rivalry on TV and around the

Internet? That the crowd seemed more vocal at both Yankee Stadium and at Fenway Park when these teams played each other? Did I just fall into line as easily as a crowd of people does when the big video screen at a ballpark flashes up a message to "MAKE! SOME! NOISE!"? Or is it because in my home county of Lincolnshire, there's a hamlet called New York about a twenty-minute drive from a town called Boston, and they've always hated each other? (That's probably not true; I've never been to New York, Lincs.)

How do I go from not knowing anything about the Red Sox, other than that they are in the same division as the team I liked, to deliberately taking the long way out of Safeco Field, against the flow of people leaving the main entrance just so I can get some yuks seeing unhappy Red Sox fans leaving the park? Why did I get an incredible amount of joy from hearing a guy on his cellphone in the car next to ours as we waited to get out of the parking lot, barking his displeasure at the Red Sox losing to "the crappy effing Mariners"?

Isn't that all completely ridiculous? Or is it just something like people having a second team that they kind of have a soft spot for?

Is rooting against a team just another form of supporting a team? Is hating the Cardinals the other side of the coin from loving the Cubs? Is it because you want to support you own team twice somehow? Or is it partly a backup plan if your own team loses or doesn't make the playoffs? Is it just some sort of second-best quick shag in an alley with a random person you met in a bar just to feel like you accomplished something?

In June 2010, I went to three games at the SkyDome, to see the Yankees play the Blue Jays. I cheered while Jays fans booed A-Rod. I clapped for every throw to first that a Yankee pitcher made, throws that naturally got booed by home team's fans. Somewhere around me at one of those three games, there must've been a Red Sox fan rooting for the Jays, rooting against the Yankees, and spitting bile about that idiot guy with the Jeter jersey down there who stood up cheering Brett Gardner's triple.

My soft-spot team is the Rockies. You wanna know why? Four things combined to make me like them: first, I was rooting for them in the 2007 World Series (of course); second, I saw them hit four solo home runs against the White Sox at U.S. Cellular Field and still lose 5–4; third, I had an utterly fantastic night at Coors Field meeting an email friend for the very first time, and got to see my first live inside-the-park home run; finally, I kinda like that they are aesthetically the anti-Yankees. Whether you love or hate the Yankees, they have undeniably classy uniforms. I can live without that stars-and-stripes top-hat logo, but everything else looks cool and you know it will look cool in another hundred, two hundred, five hundred years. The same cannot be said about the Rockies, and perversely, inexplicably, I love them for it.

DETROIT TIGERS
A DEDICATED FAN'S SUMMER

TIGERS

WORK

SLEEP

OTHER STUFF

DETROIT TIGERS SEASON
APRIL 6–OCTOBER 6, 2009

The 2009 Detroit Tigers season ran from Monday, April 6, to Tuesday, October 6. That's 163 games in 184 days.
The total duration of those 163 games was 27,582 minutes, or 19 days 3 hours and 42 minutes.

According to the U.S. Department of Labor, the average American works a 7-hour 35.4-minute day. Assuming that this same average American works a five-day week, that's 58,747 minutes of the 129 weekdays of the Tigers' season (132 days minus Memorial Day, Independence Day, and Labor Day).

The University of Maryland Medical Center says the average person sleeps 7.5 hours a night.

So, an average American who also happens to be a well-above-average Tigers fan, a fan who watches *every* minute of every game, would spend 10.4% of the baseball season watching his or her team; that's 5.5% of the whole year before you even add spring training, the All-Star Game, and the postseason. And were this person also a Lions, Pistons, and Red Wings fan, well, he'd barely have time to poop.

WASHINGTON, D.C.

EXACTLY HOW MANY TEAMS CALLED THE NATIONALS/SENATORS DOES ONE CITY NEED?

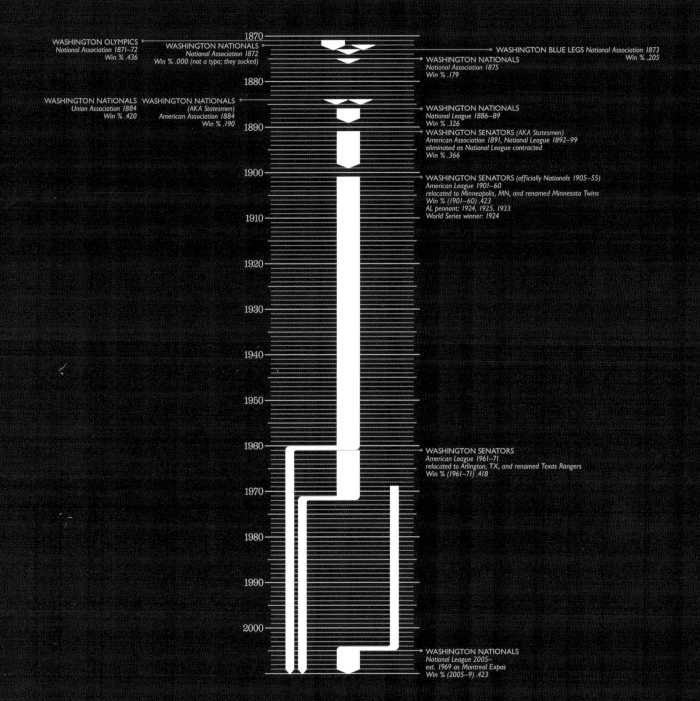

WASHINGTON OLYMPICS
National Association 1871–72
Win % .436

WASHINGTON NATIONALS
National Association 1872
Win % .000 (not a typo; they sucked)

WASHINGTON BLUE LEGS *National Association 1873*
Win % .205

WASHINGTON NATIONALS
National Association 1875
Win % .179

WASHINGTON NATIONALS
Union Association 1884
Win % .420

WASHINGTON NATIONALS
(AKA Statesmen)
American Association 1884
Win % .190

WASHINGTON NATIONALS
National League 1886–89
Win % .326

WASHINGTON SENATORS *(AKA Statesmen)*
American Association 1891, National League 1892–99
eliminated as National League contracted
Win % .366

WASHINGTON SENATORS *(officially Nationals 1905–55)*
American League 1901–60
relocated to Minneapolis, MN, and renamed Minnesota Twins
Win % (1901–60) .423
AL pennant: 1924, 1925, 1933
World Series winner: 1924

WASHINGTON SENATORS
American League 1961–71
relocated to Arlington, TX, and renamed Texas Rangers
Win % (1961–71) .418

WASHINGTON NATIONALS
National League 2005–
est. 1969 as Montreal Expos
Win % (2005–9) .423

WASHINGTON, DISTRICT OF COLUMBIA, THE CAPITAL OF THE UNITED STATES. HOME TO A WHOLE HEAP OF FINE BUILDINGS, MUSEUMS, MOMUMENTS, AND THE GREAT BAND FUGAZI. ALSO HOME TO A STRING OF UNSUCCESSFUL BASEBALL TEAMS, VIRTUALLY ALL OF WHICH WERE CALLED THE SENATORS OR NATIONALS. THROUGHOUT THE HISTORY OF PROFESSIONAL BASEBALL IN D.C., THERE HAVE BEEN TWELVE TEAMS, HAVING WON A GRAND TOTAL OF THREE PENNANTS AND ONE WORLD SERIES. UP TO AND INCLUDING THE 2009 SEASON, THE COMBINED WIN-LOSS TOTALS FOR D.C. TEAMS IS 6,014–8,595; THAT'S A WIN PERCENTAGE OF .412

THERE WERE ALSO FOUR NEGRO LEAGUE TEAMS BETWEEN 1924 AND 1938. NONE OF THOSE WAS PARTICULARLY GOOD, EITHER: THEIR COLLECTIVE WIN PERCENTAGE IS .415

THOSE TEAMS WERE:
WASHINGTON POTOMACS *Independent 1923 Eastern Colored League 1924, relocated to Wilmington, DE, 1925 Win % .390*

WASHINGTON PILOTS *Negro East West League 1932 Win % .314*

WASHINGTON ELITE GIANTS *Negro National League 1936–37 est. 1920 as Nashville Standard Giants, renamed Nashville Elite Giants 1920–30, 1931–34, relocated and renamed Cleveland Cubs 1931, relocated and renamed Columbus Elite Giants 1935, relocated and renamed Baltimore Elite Giants 1938–50 Win % (1936–37) .539*

WASHINGTON BLACK SENATORS *Negro National League 1938 Win % .133*

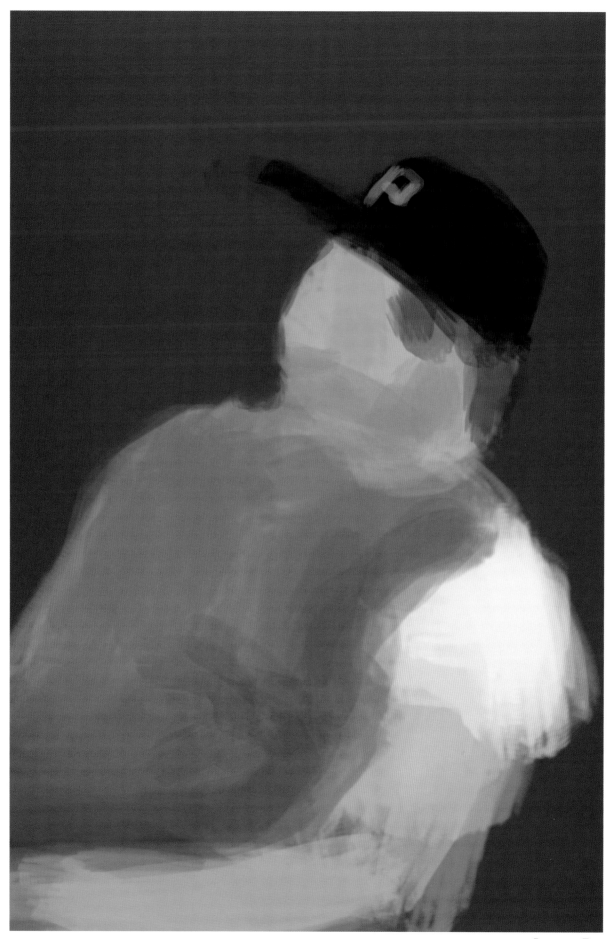

Pirates Fan

KANSAS CITY COWBOYS' 1886 SCHEDULE

Apr 30, May 1	vs. Chicago White Stockings
May 3, 5	vs. Detroit Wolverines
May 7, 8, 10	at St. Louis Maroons
May 18, 19, 20	vs. New York Giants
May 21, 22, 24	vs. Boston Beaneaters
May 27, 28, 29 (2)	at Philadelphia Quakers
June 1	at Washington Nationals
June 2, 3, 4	at New York Giants
June 5, 7, 8	at Boston Beaneaters
June 11, 12, 14	at Chicago White Stockings
June 15, 16, 17	at Detroit Wolverines
June 19, 21, 22	vs. St. Louis Maroons
June 23, 24	vs. Boston Beaneaters
June 28, 29, 30	vs. New York Giants
July 1, 2, 3	vs. Philadelphia Quakers
July 5 (2), 6	vs. Washington Nationals
July 8, 9, 10	vs. St. Louis Maroons
July 12, 13, 14	vs. Detroit Wolverines
July 15, 16, 17	vs. Chicago White Stockings
July 19, 20, 21	vs. Detroit Wolverines
July 22, 23, 24	at Chicago White Stockings
July 28, 29, 30	at Philadelphia Quakers
July 31, Aug 2, 3	at Washington Nationals
Aug 4, 5, 6	at New York Giants
Aug 7, 9, 10	at Boston Beaneaters
Aug 12, 13, 14	at Detroit Wolverines
Aug 16, 17, 18	at Chicago White Stockings
Aug 20, 21, 23	at St. Louis Maroons
Aug 24, 25, 26	vs. New York Giants
Aug 27, 28, 30, 31	vs. Washington Nationals
Sept 1, 2, 3, 4	vs. Philadelphia Quakers
Sept 6, 7, 8	vs. Boston Beaneaters
Sept 9, 10, 11	vs. St. Louis Maroons
Sept 13, 14, 15 (2)	vs. Detroit Wolverines
Sept 16, 17 (2), 18	vs. Chicago White Stockings
Sept 20, 21, 22, 23	at St. Louis Maroons
Sept 25, 27, 28, 29	at New York Giants
Sept 30, Oct 1, 2	at Boston Beaneaters
Oct 4, 5, 6	at Philadelphia Quakers
Oct 7 (2), 8 (2), 9 (2), 11	at Washington Nationals

July 24, 25, 26	vs. Boston Red Sox
July 27, 28, 29, 30	vs Washington Senators
July 31, Aug 1, 2	vs. New York Yankees
Aug 4 (2), 5, 6	at Boston Red Sox
Aug 7, 8, 9 (2)	at New York Yankees
Aug 10, 11, 12, 13	vs. Cleveland Indians
Aug 14, 15, 16	vs. Chicago White Sox
Aug 18, 19, 20	vs. Boston Red Sox
Aug 21, 22	vs. New York Yankees
Aug 23 (2)	vs. Washington Senators
Aug 25, 26	vs. Baltimore Orioles
Aug 28, 29, 30	vs. Detroit Tigers
Sept 2	at Cleveland Indians
Sept 4, 5, 6	at Detroit Tigers
Sept 7 (2), 8	at Chicago White Sox
Sept 9, 10	at New York Yankees
Sept 11, 12	at Boston Red Sox
Sept 13 (2), 14	at Baltimore Orioles
Sept 15 (2)	at Washington Senators
Sept 18, 19, 20	vs. Cleveland Indians
Sept 22, 23	at Detroit Tigers
Sept 25 (2), 26, 27	at Cleveland Indians

KANSAS CITY ATHLETICS' 1959 SCHEDULE

Apr 10, 11	vs. Cleveland Indians
Apr 14, 15, 16	at Chicago White Sox
Apr 17, 18, 19	at Cleveland Indians
Apr 21, 22	vs. Chicago White Sox
Apr 24, 25, 26	vs. Detroit Tigers
Apr 28, 29	vs. Washington Senators
Apr 30, May 1, 2	vs. Baltimore Orioles
May 3, 4	vs. Boston Red Sox
May 5, 6	vs. New York Yankees
May 8, 9, 10	at Detroit Tigers
May 14	at Baltimore Orioles
May 15, 16	at Washington Senators
May 17 (2)	at New York Yankees
May 20, 21	at Boston Red Sox
May 22, 23, 24	vs. Chicago White Sox
May 25, 26	vs. Detroit Tigers
May 28, 30 (2)	at Cleveland Indians
May 31, June 1	at Chicago White Sox
June 2, 3, 4	vs. Boston Red Sox
June 5, 6, 7	vs. Baltimore Orioles
June 9, 10, 11	at New York Yankees
June 12, 13, 14	at Boston Red Sox
June 15, 17, 18	at Washington Senators
June 19 (2), 20, 21	at Baltimore Orioles
June 22, 23, 24, 25	vs. New York Yankees
June 26, 27, 28	vs. Washington Senators
June 29, 30, July 1	at Detroit Tigers
July 2, 3	vs. Cleveland Indians
July 4 (2), 5	vs. Chicago White Sox
July 9 (2), 10	vs. Detroit Tigers
July 11, 12 (2)	at Chicago White Sox
July 14 (2), 16	at Baltimore Orioles
July 17, 18, 19 (2)	at Washington Senators
July 21, 22, 23	vs. Baltimore Orioles

KANSAS CITY ROYALS' 2009 SCHEDULE

Apr 6, 8, 9	at Chicago White Sox
Apr 10, 11, 12	vs. Yankees
Apr 13, 14, 15	vs. Indians
Apr 17, 18, 19	at Texas Rangers
Apr 21, 22, 23	at Cleveland Indians
Apr 24, 25, 26	vs. Detroit Tigers
Apr 27, 28, 29, 30	vs. Toronto Blue Jays
May 1, 2, 3	at Minnesota Twins
May 4, 5	vs. Chicago White Sox
May 6, 7	vs. Seattle Mariners
May 8, 9, 10	at Los Angeles Angels of Anaheim
May 12, 13	at Oakland Athletics
May 14, 15, 16, 17	vs. Baltimore Orioles
May 19, 20, 21	vs. Cleveland Indians
May 22, 23, 24	at St. Louis Cardinals
May 25, 26, 27	vs. Detroit Tigers
May 29, 30, 31	vs. Chicago White Sox
June 2, 3, 4	at Tampa Bay Rays
June 5, 6, 7	at Toronto Blue Jays
June 9, 10, 11	at Cleveland Indians
June 12, 13, 14	vs. Cincinnati Red
June 16, 17, 18	vs. Arizona Diamondbacks
June 19, 20, 21	vs. St. Louis Cardinals
June 23, 24, 25	at Houston Astros
June 26, 27, 28	at Pittsburgh Pirates
June 29, 30, July 1	vs. Minnesota Twins
July 2, 3, 4, 5	vs. Chicago White Sox
July 6, 7, 8	at Detroit Tigers
July 9, 10, 11, 12	at Boston Red Sox
July 17, 18, 19	vs. Tampa Bay Rays
July 20, 21, 22	vs. Los Angeles Angels of Anaheim
July 24, 25, 26	vs. Texas Rangers
July 27, 28, 29, 30	at Baltimore Orioles
July 31, Aug 1, 2, 3	at Tampa Bay Rays
Aug 4, 5, 6	vs. Seattle Mariners
Aug 7, 8, 9	vs. Oakland Athletics
Aug 11, 12, 13	at Minnesota Twins
Aug 14, 15, 16	at Detroit Tigers
Aug 17, 18, 19	at Chicago White Sox
Aug 21, 22, 23	vs. Minnesota Twins
Aug 24, 25, 26	vs. Cleveland Indians
Aug 27, 28, 29, 30	at Seattle Mariners
Aug 31, Sept 1, 2	at Oakland Athletics
Sept 4, 5, 6, 7	vs. Los Angeles Angels of Anaheim
Sept 8, 9, 10	vs. Detroit Tigers
Sept 11, 12, 13	at Cleveland Indians
Sept 15, 16, 17	at Detroit Tigers
Sept 18, 19, 20	at Chicago White Sox
Sept 21, 22, 23, 24	vs. Boston Red Sox
Sept 25, 26, 27	vs. Minnesota Twins
Sept 28, 29, 30	at New York Yankees
Oct 2, 3, 4	at Minnesota Twins

KANSAS CITY COWBOYS' TRAVEL SCHEDULE 1886
(APPROX. 8,400 MILES)
KANSAS CITY ATHLETICS' TRAVEL SCHEDULE 1959
(APPROX. 18,000 MILES)
KANSAS CITY ROYALS' TRAVEL SCHEDULE 2009
(APPROX. 26,800 MILES)

CLEVELAND INDIANS
OH, REALLY?

■ NATIVE AMERICAN POPULATION OF CLEVELAND, OHIO
■ NON–NATIVE AMERICAN POPULATION OF CLEVELAND, OHIO

"O CANADA"
HOW OFTEN HAVE THE EXPOS AND BLUE JAYS HEARD ONLY "O CANADA" BEFORE A GAME

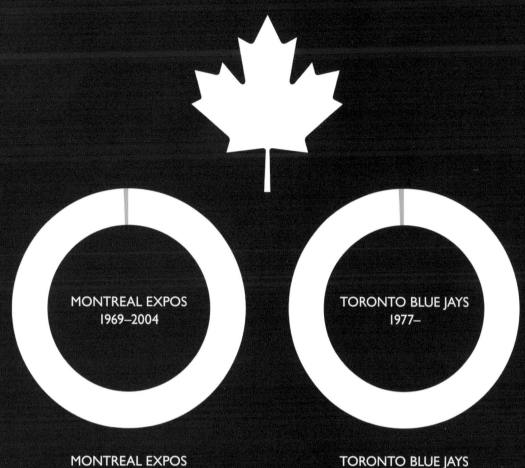

MONTREAL EXPOS
1969–2004

TORONTO BLUE JAYS
1977–

MONTREAL EXPOS

TOTAL GAMES: 5,708[1]
GAMES AGAINST BLUE JAYS: 43
GAMES AGAINST BLUE JAYS IN CANADA: 40[4]

TORONTO BLUE JAYS

TOTAL GAMES: 5,265[2, 3]
GAMES AGAINST EXPOS: 43
GAMES AGAINST EXPOS IN CANADA: 40[4]

ONLY 0.701% OF EXPOS GAMES AND 0.759% OF BLUE JAYS GAMES WERE PLAYED
WHERE THE ONLY NATIONAL ANTHEM HEARD WAS "O CANADA."
WHEN THE TEAMS PLAYED THREE GAMES IN PUERTO RICO, THE ANTHEMS
OF PUERTO RICO, THE UNITED STATES, AND CANADA WERE PLAYED.
THAT'S ONE IN EVERY 269 GAMES PLAYED BY THE EXPOS OR JAYS UP TO THE END OF 2008.

[1] Including 10 postseason games
[2] Including 41 postseason games
[3] Total games to the end of the 2009 season
[4] Three of the Expos–Blue Jays interleague games were played in San Juan, Puerto Rico, July 2–4, 2004

eMb
LES EXPOS DE MONTRÉAL

'69 '70 '71 '72 '73 '74 '75 '76 '77 '78 '79 '80 '81 '82 '83 '84 '85 '86 '87 '88 '89 '90 '91 '92 '93 '94 '95 '96 '97 '98 '99 '00 '01 '02 '03 '04

OWNERS
CHARLES BRONFMAN — CLAUDE BROCHU — JEFFREY LORIA — EXPOS BASEBALL LP

GENERAL MANAGERS
JIM FANNING — CHARLIE FOX ▼ — JOHN McHALE — BILL STONEMAN ▼ — MURRAY COOK — DAN DUQUETTE ▼ — DAVE DOMBROWSKI — KEVIN MALONE ▲ — LARRY BEINFEST (INTERIM GM) ▼ — JIM BEATTIE — OMAR MINAYA

MANAGERS
GENE MAUCH — KARL KUEHL ▼ — DICK WILLIAMS — ▲ CHARLIE FOX — JIM FANNING — JIM FANNING ▼ — ▲ BILL VIRDON — BUCK RODGERS — TOM RUNNELLS ▼ — FELIPE ALOU — JEFF TORBORG ▼ — FRANK ROBINSON

WIN-LOSS PERCENTAGE
.600
.500
.400
.321 .441 .449 .451 .488 .491 .463 .340 .463 .469 .594 .556 .556 .531 .506 .484 .484 .522 .562 .500 .500 .525 .441 .537 .580 .649 .458 .543 .481 .401 .420 .414 .420 .512 .512 .414

POSITION IN NATIONAL LEAGUE EAST

PLAYOFFS
NLDS — EXPOS 3, PHILLIES 2
NLCS — DODGERS 3, EXPOS 2

ATTENDANCE (AND RANK IN NATIONAL LEAGUE)

Attendance	Rank
1,212,608	7/12
1,424,683	6/9
1,290,963	8/12
1,142,145	6/12
1,246,863	6/12
1,019,134	6/12
908,292	6/12
646,704	11/12
1,433,757	6/12
1,427,007	7/12
2,102,173	4/12
2,208,175	4/12
1,534,564	3/12
2,318,292	3/12
2,320,651	2/12
1,606,531	8/12
1,502,494	8/12
1,128,981	11/12
1,850,324	9/12
1,478,659	11/12
1,783,533	10/01
1,373,087	10/12
934,742	12/12
1,669,127	10/12
1,641,437	13/14
1,276,250	11/14
1,309,618	14/14
1,616,709	11/14
1,497,609	13/14
914,909	16/16
773,277	16/16
926,272	16/16
642,745	16/16
812,045	16/16
1,025,639	16/16
749,550	16/16

BALLPARKS
JARRY PARK STADIUM — OLYMPIC STADIUM — HIRAM BITHORN STADIUM, SAN JUAN, PUERTO RICO (22 HOME GAMES IN BOTH '03. & '04') ▲

ALL STAR EXPOS
1 1 1 1 1 2 1 1 1 1 3 3 3 4 5 3 3 3 1 2 2 2 1 2 5 1 3 1 2 1 2 1

MVP: CARTER — MVP: CARTER — MVP: CARTER — MVP: RAINES

SIGH

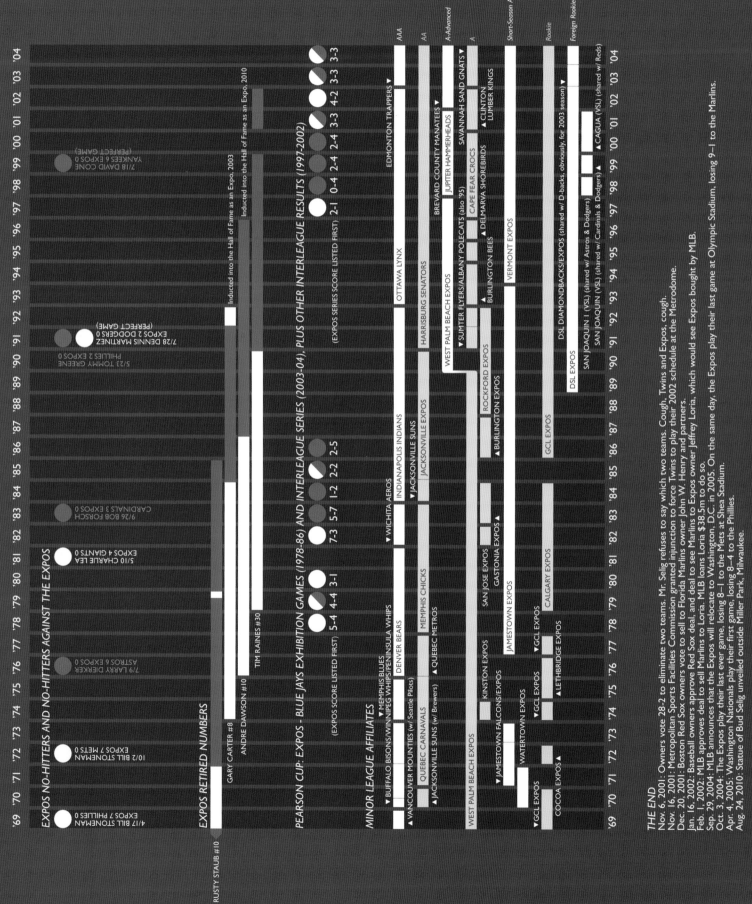

THE END

Nov. 6, 2001: Owners vote 28-2 to eliminate two teams. Mr. Selig refuses to say which two teams. Cough, Twins and Expos, cough.

Nov. 16, 2001: Metropolitan Sports Facilities Commission granted injunction to force Twins to play their 2002 schedule at the Metrodome.

Dec. 20, 2001: Boston Red Sox owners vote to sell to Florida Marlins owner John W. Henry and partners.

Jan. 16, 2002: Baseball owners approve Red Sox deal, and deal to see Marlins to Expos owner Jeffrey Loria, which would see Expos bought by MLB.

Feb. 1, 2002: MLB approves deal to sell Marlins to Loria. MLB loans Loria $38.5m to do so.

Sep. 29, 2004: MLB announces that the Expos will relocate to Washington, D.C. in 2005.

Oct. 3, 2004: The Expos play their last ever game, losing 8–1 to the Mets at Shea Stadium.

Apr. 4, 2005: Washington Nationals play their first game, losing 8–4 to the Phillies.

Aug. 24, 2010: Statue of Bud Selig unveiled outside Miller Park, Milwaukee.

SUMMER AT THE SKYDOME

I had no intention of spending my summer in Toronto. No disrespect to the Blue Jays, but in my short baseball-watching life, they've never been more than that team in Canada, the anomaly. They're the team that usually finishes below the Yankees and Red Sox in the AL East, the team that plays on that funny-looking artificial turf, and at best—until the end of the 2009 season—the reason that I'd hope the schedule would fall in such a way so that the Yanks avoided Roy Halladay as much as possible.

Before we go on, if you have a stopwatch, please start it now. I'll explain later. Thanks.

My original plan did include a visit to Toronto, but only for one game. Then I'd spend my summer moving around the States: see a few games at Yankee Stadium, visit Camden Yards again, see some ballparks that I'd not been to before, go to Cooperstown, catch a few minor league games. A nice big American summer where—in my head—I'd've been the English baseball fan equivalent of Hunter S. Thompson, speeding from Ohio to Missouri, high on mescaline, to get to a Cardinals day game after a night drinking with Indians fans. It would've been awesome. Possibly.

But then I was denied a visa to travel to the States. Sigh. Thankfully, though, Major League Baseball had seen fit to stick a team in Canada. (I know, Expos fans, I know . . .) Some emails later and I'd sorted out a place to stay where I had easy access to watching baseball all summer long. Baseball on Astroturf, baseball in a weird venue, baseball in a country where it wasn't the national pastime, but it was Major League Baseball and the U.S. consulate had decreed that I could not be picky about where I got my kicks.

So, Canada. The second-largest country in the world (by area). Toronto. Canada's largest city, the fifth-largest in North America. SkyDome. The world's first stadium with a fully retractable roof. SkyDome. Officially called something else, which shall not be mentioned here out of respect to the Torontonians I've met who never call it anything other than SkyDome. (I've slipped a couple of times and used its current name, and on more than one occasion I've been looked at the way one would expect to be looked at after showing some Danish cartoons to a fella in a Baghdad café.) In fact, the only time I ever hear the new name used is by Buck Martinez on the Jays' broadcasts on the TV channel owned by the same parent company as the one that owns the SkyDome.

After being away from North America for ten months, I was delighted to be back. Within a couple of hours of arriving at Pearson International Airport, I'd dumped my bags and was on my way to the SkyDome with my brand-new housemates Scott and Kevin to see the Blue Jays play the Rangers. And there were two national anthems. I'd kinda forgotten that I'd be experiencing that. Back-to-back, at the start of international soccer games, anthems often sound like they are trying to out-bombast each other. Not so when you get the United States and Canada's anthems back-to-back. The former hitting all the right notes of Americanness: melodically stirring, almost mocking your ability to resist its patriotism, lyrics as unsubtle as the flag they celebrate. Following that, "O Canada" sounds like it was composed to be heard on a music box. Pretty, almost twee, a song that might as well be called "We're Not the United States." (That being said, "The Star-Spangled Banner" is now totally Pavlovian for me. No matter where I am when I hear it, it totally makes me think that baseball is about to begin.)

The SkyDome is different from the ballparks I'm used to. The concrete donuts like Riverfront and the Vet were before my time. They exist within Google Images for me. And they exist as YouTube clips of their being imploded, something I watch with alarming regularity. I'd been to

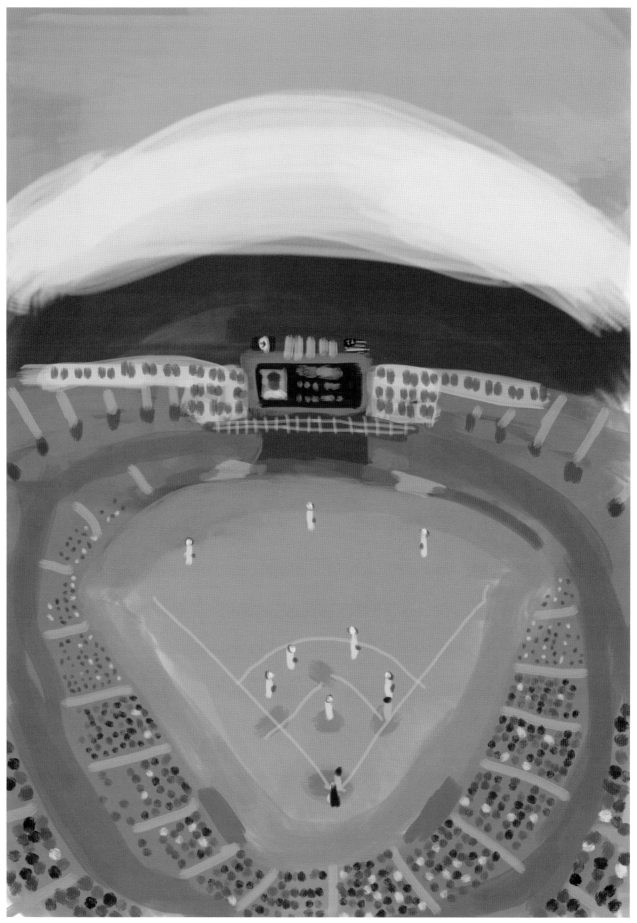

SkyDome

Shea, but that was it. And the only multipurpose venue I'd been to before the SkyDome was the Humpty Dumpty Dome in Minneapolis. But the SkyDome has a donut-esque feel. Luckily, it was a nice warm evening for that Jays-Rangers game. The roof was open. With Jays fans, the roof is a topic that comes up every time you tell someone you went to a game: was the roof open? Having subsequently gone to a couple of roof-closed games, I learned why. It's horrible. The upstairs 500 level gets all clammy and uncomfortable. It's particularly frustrating when you know that the only inclemency outdoors is that it's a little bit cloudy. And really, the average monthly precipitation during the baseball season in Toronto is fairly similar to Chicago's. I don't foresee them putting a roof on Wrigley anytime soon, do you?

So, some facts: The SkyDome opened in June 1989. It took a little bit more than two and a half years to build. The architect was some guy with a retractable pencil and quite likely a splendid set of Rotring pens. It cost $570 million to build. Taxpayers paid a significant chunk of that. In 1998, the SkyDome filed for bankruptcy protection and was bought by Sportsco International LP for $85 million. In 2004, Rogers Communications bought the SkyDome for $25 million. Below are those numbers again in the form of a graph just to ram home how absurd they are.

It's not the most attractive place to watch baseball; no amount of fondness for the city of Toronto can disguise that fact. Even if you're just watching it on TV, how many places look worse than the SkyDome? Dolphin Stadium and Tropicana Field . . . that's about it, right? But like a lot of things in life, I got used to it and started to enjoy some of the elements of the SkyDome. I like how each section of the 500 level has a different-colored entrance, so that in among the blue seats, there's a spectrum of entrances flowing from yellow above left field through oranges and reds above the first base line, pinks and purples behind home plate, and blues and greens all the way to right field. As well as that rainbow, the sky theme continues in the four exit ramps, which have clouds, suns, stars, and moons decorating the supporting concrete columns. And every time I go to the SkyDome, I find myself wondering how many other ballparks don't actually have a pole for a foul pole. In Toronto, the "poles" are just long tongues of yellow netting anchored taut.

The AstroTurf is ugly; there's no making excuses for that. There are darker and lighter rectangles all over the field. And you can still see the gridiron marks for the Canadian Football League Argonauts games. The pitcher's mound and the home plate area aren't circular; they are hexagonal and look like they were cut out by a right-

1989: CONSTRUCTION COST $570M

1998: SOLD TO SPORTSCO INTERNATIONAL LP FOR $85M

2004: SOLD TO ROGERS COMMUNICATIONS FOR $25M

handed man using left-handed scissors. The video board is enormous, and it's surrounded by a hotel. A hotel. I occasionally fantasize while sweating in the 500-level sun about how it would be nice to rent a room, turn up the AC to cool down, order some room service, and watch the game through the window, eating french fries out of one of those linen bundles that they come in in hotels. Most of the time, though, all I can think about when I see the hotel (especially when the roof is closed) is an image that I wish my brain had never conjured up: Roger Clemens at one o'clock in the morning, the night before one of his starts, naked and erect, staring down at the mound, psyching himself up through gritted teeth: "You are the best, Rocket! You! Are! The! Best!"

While I'm on the topic of the aesthetics of watching the Blue Jays: the uniforms. That cap logo, the "Jays" on the chest—market-researched into an ugly lack of personality that is painful to see on fans. Even the steroid-y pumped-up blue-jay-with-biceps logo of the early 2000s is better than this one. There's the black alternate jerseys, too. And the lazily designed "T" on the road caps . . . It's even sadder because of the beauty of their earlier logo: the beautiful, graphically strong blue jay's head over a baseball with a maple leaf offset to the side. Thankfully, though, the team wore their throwback powder blues for a few of the games I went to and, somewhat interestingly, the powder blue looked fantastic against the green artificial turf.

Imperfections notwithstanding, the SkyDome was my baseball home for three months. I saw more than half of the Blue Jays' home games during that period. I saw them play more in three months than I've ever seen my favorite team play. It was a new experience to watch a team so frequently. Seeing a good day at the plate, seeing golden sombreros. Seeing some great double plays and some comedic errors. Seeing Ricky Romero pitch solidly virtually every time, and wondering if the bullpen would cough up a defeat and erase Ricky's double-u. And all those home runs. In the thirty-two games I went to, I saw the Blue Jays hit sixty-nine home runs (including sixteen by Jose Bautista). As a friend of mine reminds me when he reports on his Ortiz-like nights playing softball, chicks dig the long ball.

But not that many of those chicks (or dudes, for that matter) are around in Toronto, it would seem. Apart from when the Yankees or Red Sox were in town, the attendance was fairly underwhelming. There were only 14,079 there to see Albert Pujols go 4 for 5. In late May when the Rays were looking invincible, only 11,355 turned out to see the best team in the league play the league's home run leaders. But, as everyone kept telling me, Torontonians care more about hockey. The apathy makes me feel for the die-hard Jays fans, the ones you see at all the games. It's far much more fun cheering on your team when there's a lot of you. But one of the lesser-noted benefits of sparse crowds is that there's less chance of the wave working (not that it stops people trying, though).

My formative baseball experiences were at the old Yankee Stadium, where the PA announcements of the late Bob Sheppard were beautifully calm and simple: *Now batting for the Yankees, number two, Derek Jeter.* It turns out you're not supposed to do it with understated style and grace, oh no. You need to do it like the Skydome's announcer, Tim Langton, does it: Lyle . . . . Oooooooooooooooooooooooooh-verbay. Langton, according to his website, is a professional voice talent. (I wonder if that's what he says if you meet him at a party. "Hi, my name's Tim, I'm a professional voice talent." Maybe he just flips into announcer mode and says, "Tim . . . . Laaaaaaaaaaangton.") If there's one thing that grinds my gears at Blue Jays games, it's him. I'm not naïve enough to think that all announcers are Bob Sheppard, and I know sometimes a goofy cheerleader can rev up the crowd, but Langton is just so bad at it. He clearly wants to give each player a signature call, but aside from Overbay, none of the players' names is particularly good for that. He resorts to leaving a big gap between given name and surname.

It takes him 3.13 seconds to announce Fred Lewis; 1.06 seconds of that is the gap between his names. With John Buck, the gap is 0.91 seconds, which accounts for 49.4 percent of the whole call. And the elongated "O" of Overbay takes up 29.2 percent of his whole name when Langton says it.

I love the little things you notice when you go to the same ballpark regularly. I love it when I go to a game with my friend Scott, a longtime Jays fan, who does the same thing every time he sees one particular program vendor.

"Hey, Ralph," Scott will shout.

Ralph will look around and see Scott, and he'll have a quizzical look on his face. Scott will remind Ralph that he used to work part-time at Exhibition Stadium.

In a way that says *I don't remember you,* Ralph will say, "Oh, yeah . . ."

There's the pretty woman who'll ask for my ID each of the three times I buy beer during a game, even though we had a brief conversation about my British ID the first time. (Although, after I didn't see her for a couple of months, she served me toward the end of my visit to Toronto and remembered me clearly. And didn't ID me.)

There's a guy in his twenties in an Expos hat with someone's autograph on it, always sitting with an older woman who gets way too excited at the merest hint of a fly ball.

There's a guy who sits in the 500s who completely perplexes me. He shouts to/at the players by name: "Hi,

Aaron Hill." Every player, on both teams. He's got a whiny voice, so it's difficult to make out exactly what he's saying, but the sparsity of the crowd even allows you to hear him when you're watching a Jays game on TV. I wonder what his story is. Is he trying to get a roll call going like the Bleacher Creatures at Yankee Stadium? If so, he's got a fair way to go; no one joins in, and at every game, you'll always hear a couple of voice shouting at him to shut up. (I met Andrew Stoeten of DrunkJaysFans.com, and he tells me that the shouty guy is called Andrew and not only does this at Jays games but also has been seen at the Toronto Maple Leafs training camp doing the same thing there.)

There's the rheumy-eyed old fella who sat a couple of seats away from me (I bought a partial season plan for the same 500-level seat, above first base). He's got a full season ticket because, he said, after his wife died, "What else am I gonna do with my time?"

These regulars are more noticeable, I think, because of the amount of empty seats. "Let's go Blue Jays" chants start up and peter out, as the P.A. thumps out the Addams Family theme to create some "atmosphere." (Incidentally, when the Yankees were in town, the "Yankees suck" chants spread so much more quickly than the pro-Jays chants did.)

It was nice to become more accustomed to another team's fan base just a wee bit. I've even come to quite like the goofy "OK Blue Jays" song that they play in the seventh-inning stretch (it got to number 47 on the Canadian charts in 1983 and has truly awful lyrics).

The biggest joy of my Blue Jay summer, though, is perfectly simple, and it can be found at any major league park: a .400 team *could* beat a .600 team; that pitcher with an ERA over 6.00 could beat Chris Carpenter; that weak-hitting shortstop could hit four home runs. At every single game, I go in thinking these kind of things. In my head, both pitchers are going to throw perfect games until they eventually give up a hit or a walk. And even if something extraordinary doesn't happen, I'll be seeing a baseball game. There is no such thing as a boring game. I saw exciting games with a bunch of home runs, as well as magnificent pitching duels; I saw the Jays beat each of that day's American League division leaders. The greatest moments, though, were games where I simply did not care about the result. Games that I happened to have a ticket for and went to a little halfheartedly, buying a beer and some peanuts and sitting there on my own, getting into the game, thinking about shit, watching groundouts to short, easy pop-ups, and bloop singles, and (I don't know why this still amazes me) suddenly being very aware that I cared about this game, and I care about the game. I love the SkyDome for that, just as I love Coors Field, U.S. Cellular, PNC Park, and Petco Park; just, in fact, as I love the baseball field at Rennbahnstrasse in Berlin, where, after playing a game with the Prenzlauer Berg Piranhas, some teammates and I would hang around to watch the next game between some crazy mixture of American, German, Hispanic, and Japanese players. Baseball is magic. Doesn't really matter where it's played. Sure, it's more aesthetically pleasing if it's at Wrigley or Fenway, but I'm sure it may even be magic at Tropicana Field. The cowbells would drive me nuts, but that'd be when I became that guy who listens to the radio commentary on headphones at a game.

Right, you know how at the beginning of this chunk of text, I asked you to start your stopwatch? Stop it now, please. What number you got? Well, that's pretty much the exact amount of time it took Blue Jays manager Cito Gaston to walk from the dugout to the mound. I love Cito. He was pretty much my favorite thing about the Blue Jays over the summer. He just always looks so relaxed, even when he maybe shouldn't. The Jays could be up 15–1 in the fifth or down 6–4 with two outs and a runner on second in the ninth, and his calm expression never seems to change. Watching the Jays on TV, when the camera shows Cito sitting in the dugout, you could CGI out the background and replace it with a Hawaiian beachfront café and his posture wouldn't look out of place. When he's looking at scouting reports and whatnot in a folder, I just imagine it's a menu and he's about to order some spicy BBQ wings. When he saunters up the dugout steps, signals that he wants a righty from the bullpen, and strolls to the mound, he does it in the same way that I imagine him leaving his beach lounger and strolling over to the bar to get a piña colada served in a coconut shell full of swirly straws. In my head, he's not wearing the Jays uniform; he's wearing a Speedo and an ankle bracelet. But that's just in my head. Really, he's walking to the mound to hand the ball over to a righty who'll blowtorch a two-run lead and leave Ricky Romero with a no-decision.

ALL-AMERICAN GIRLS PROFESSIONAL BASEBALL LEAGUE
DUDES DIG THE LONG BALL, TOO

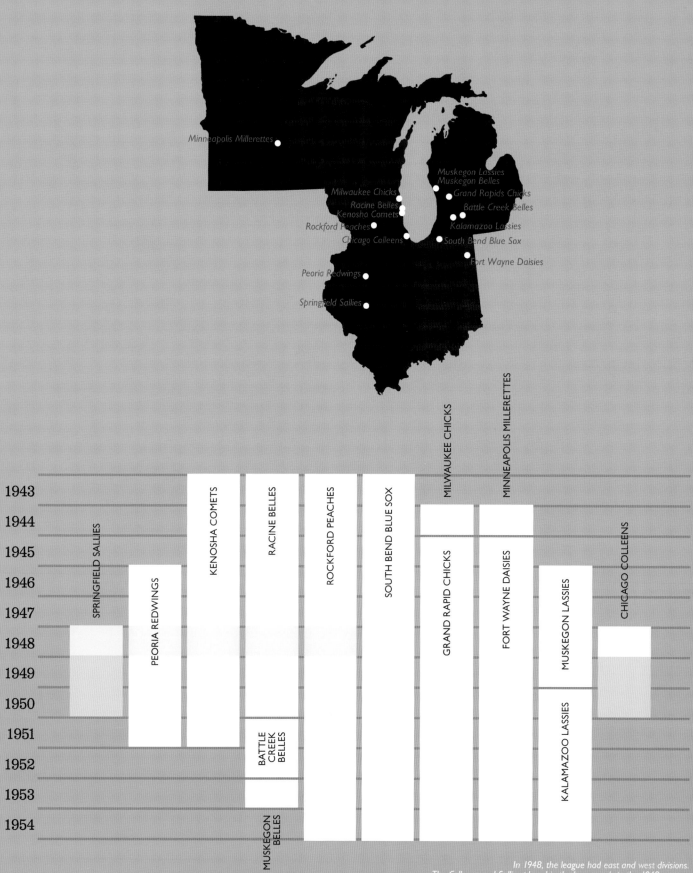

Minneapolis Millerettes

Muskegon Lassies
Muskegon Belles
Milwaukee Chicks
Grand Rapids Chicks
Racine Belles
Kenosha Comets
Battle Creek Belles
Rockford Peaches
Kalamazoo Lassies
Chicago Colleens
South Bend Blue Sox
Peoria Redwings
Fort Wayne Daisies
Springfield Sallies

MILWAUKEE CHICKS
MINNEAPOLIS MILLERETTES

1943
1944
1945
1946
1947
1948
1949
1950
1951
1952
1953
1954

SPRINGFIELD SALLIES
PEORIA REDWINGS
KENOSHA COMETS
RACINE BELLES
ROCKFORD PEACHES
SOUTH BEND BLUE SOX
GRAND RAPID CHICKS
FORT WAYNE DAISIES
MUSKEGON LASSIES
KALAMAZOO LASSIES
CHICAGO COLLEENS
BATTLE CREEK BELLES
MUSKEGON BELLES

In 1948, the league had east and west divisions.
The Colleens and Sallies played in the league only in the 1948 season;
they were development teams playing exhibition games for the following two seasons.

PACIFIC COAST LEAGUE

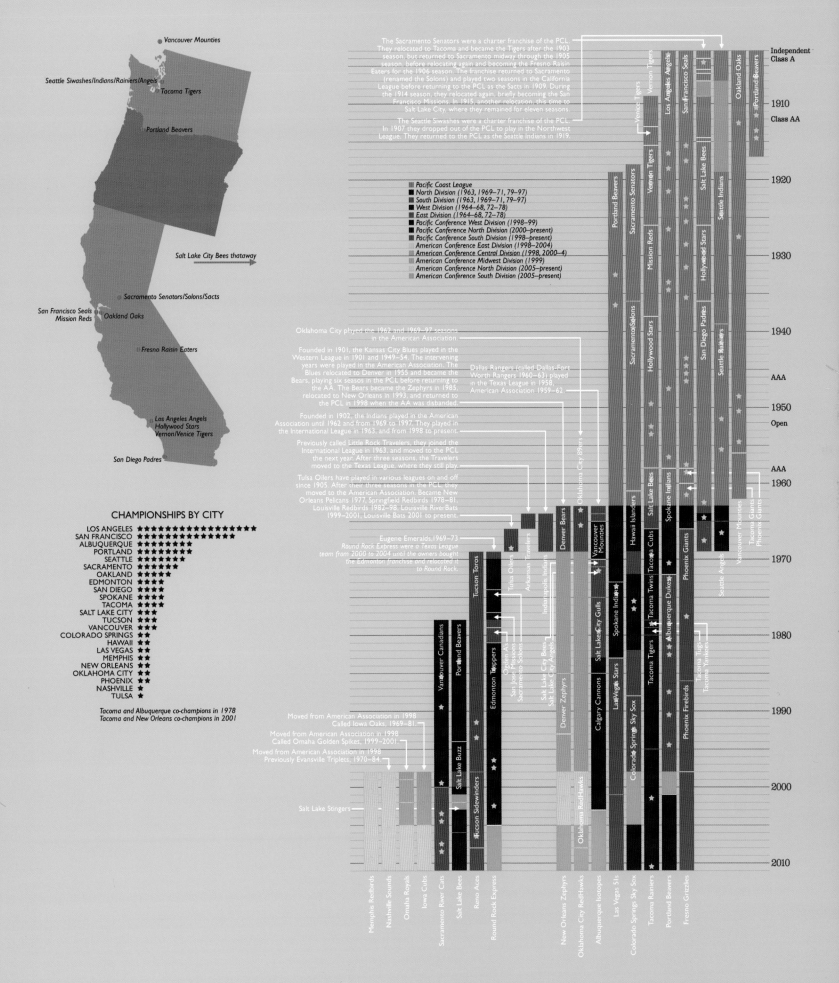

Vancouver Canadians (OAK)
Everett AquaSox (SEA)
Tacoma Rainiers (SEA)
Spokane Indians (TEX)
Yakima Bears (ARI)
Great Falls Voyagers (CWS)
Tri-City Dust Devils (COL)
Missoula Osprey (ARI)
Portland Beavers (SD)
Yakima Brewers (MIL)
Salem-Keizer Volcanoes (SF)
Eugene Emeralds (SD)
Boise Hawks (CHC)
Idaho Falls Chukars (KC)
Casper Ghosts (COL)
Ogden Raptors (LAD)
Reno Aces (ARI)
Salt Lake Bees (LAA)
Sacramento River Cats (OAK)
Orem Owlz (LAA)
San Jose Giants (SF)
Stockton Ports (OAK)
Modesto Nuts (COL)
Fresno Grizzlies (SF)
Colorado Srpings Sky Sox (COL)
Visalia Rawhide (ARI)
Bakersfield Blaze (TEX)
Las Vegas 51s (TOR)
Lancaster JetHawks (HOU)
High Desert Mavericks (SEA)
Rancho Cucamonga Quakes (LAA)
Inland Empire 66ers of San Bernadina (LAD)
Lake Elsinore Storm (SD)
Albuquerque Isotopes (LAD)
AZL Mariners, AZL Padres   AZL Athletics, AZL Brewers
AZL Rangers, AZL Royals
AZL Dodgers   AZL Giants
AZL Indians   AZL Cubs
AZL Angels

AAA	●	International League
AAA	●	Pacific Coast League
AA	●	Texas League
AA	●	Southern League
AA	○	Eastern League
A-Advanced	●	California League
A-Advanced	●	Carolina League
A-Advanced	●	Florida State League
A	●	South Atlantic League
A	●	Midwest League
A Short-Season	●	Northwest League
A Short-Season	●	New York-Penn League
Advanced Rookie	●	Pioneer Baseball League
Advanced Rookie	●	Appalachian League
Rookie	●	Arizona League
Rookie	○	Gulf Coast League

MINOR LEAGUE BASEBALL
TEAMS AND LOCATIONS 2010

Vermont Lake Monsters (WAS)

Portland Sea Dogs (BOS)

New Hampshire Fisher Cats (TOR)

Lowell Spinners (BOS)

Tri-City ValleyCats (HOU)

Rochester Red Wings (MIN)

Syracuse Chiefs (WAS)

Auburn Doubledays (TOR)

Pawtucket Red Sox (BOS)

Wisconsin Timber Rattlers (MIL)

Great Lake Loons (LAD)

Batavia Muckdogs (STL)

Buffalo Bisons (NYM)

New Britain Rock Cats (MIN)

Connecticut Tigers (DET)

Binghampton Mets (NYM)

Hudson Valley Renegades (TB)

West Michigan Whitecaps (DET)

Lansing Lugnuts (TOR)

Erie SeaWolves (DET)

Jamestown Jammers (FLA)

Scranton/Wilkes-Barre Yankees (NYY)

Beloit Snappers (MIN)

Lake County Captains (CLE)

Williamsport Crosscutters (PHI)

Staten Island Yankees (NYY)

Brooklyn Cyclones (NYM)

Kane County Cougars (OAK)

Toledo Mud Hens (DET)

Mahoning Valley Scrappers (CLE)

Lehigh Valley IronPigs (PHI)

Trenton Thunder (NYY)

Cedar Rapids Kernels (LAA)

Clinton LumberKings (SEA)

South Bend Silver Hawks (ARI)

Altoona Curve (PIT)

Reading Phillies (PHI)

Lakewood BlueClaws (PHI)

Akron Aeros (CLE)

State College Spikes (PIT)

Harrisburg Senators (WAS)

Iowa Cubs (CHC)

Quad Cities River Bandits (STL)

Fort Wayne TinCaps (SD)

Wilmington Blue Rocks (KC)

Omaha Royals (KC)

Aberdeen IronBirds (BAL)

Burlington Bees (KC)

Peoria Chiefs (CHC)

Frederick Keys (BAL)

Bowie BaySox (BAL)

Columbus Clippers (CLE)

Dayton Dragons (CIN)

Indianapolis Indians (PIT)

Potomac Nationals (WAS)

Delmarva Shorebirds (BAL)

West Virginia Power (PIT)

Richmond Flying Squirrels (SF)

Louisville Bats (CIN)

Lynchburg Hillcats (CIN)

Norfolk Tides (BAL)

Lexington Legends (HOU)

Salem Red Sox (BOS)

Princeton Rays

Bluefield Orioles

Pulaski Mariners

Danville Braves

Springfield Cardinals (STL)

Bowling Green Hot Rods (TB)

Bristol White Sox

Kingsport Mets

Winston-Salem Dash (CWS)

Burlington Royals

Durham Bulls (TB)

Elizabethton Twins

Greensboro Grasshoppers (FLA)

Carolina Mudcats (CIN)

Kinston Indians (CLE)

Greeneville Astros

Johnson City Cardinals

Nashville Sounds (MIL)

Tennessee Smokies (CHC)

Hickory Crawdads (TEX)

Kannapolis Intimidators (CWS)

Asheville Tourists (COL)

Charlotte Knights (CWS)

Tulsa Drillers (COL)

Northwest Arkansas Naturals (KC)

West Tenn Diamond Jaxx (SEA)

Greenville Drive (BOS)

Oklahoma City RedHawks (TEX)

Memphis Redbirds (STL)

Chattanooga Lookouts (LAD)

Arkansas Travelers (LAA)

Huntsville Stars (MIL)

Myrtle Beach Pelicans (ATL)

Rome Braves (ATL)

Gwinnett Braves (ATL)

Augusta GreenJackets (SF)

Birmingham Barons (CWS)

Charleston RiverDogs (NYY)

Frisco RoughRiders (TEX)

Savannah Sand Gnats (NYM)

Mississippi Braves (ATL)

Montgomery Biscuits (TB)

Midland RockHounds (OAK)

Jacksonville Suns (FLA)

Mobile BayBears (ARI)

Round Rock Express (HOU)

Daytona Cubs (CHC)

San Antonio Missions (SD)

New Orleans Zephyrs (FLA)

GCL Braves

Brevard County Manatees (MIL), GCL Nationals

GCL Astros

Dunedin Blue Jays (TOR), GCL Blue Jays

Lakeland Flying Tigers (DET), GCL Tigers

Clearwater Threshers (PHI), GCL Phillies

Tampa Yankees (NYY), GCL Yankees

Bradenton Marauders (PIT), GCL Pirates

St. Lucie Mets (NYM), GCL Mets

GCL Orioles

Palm Beach Cardinals (STL), GCL Cardinals

Charlotte Stone Crabs (TB), GCL Rays

Jupiter Hammerheads (FLA), GCL Marlins

Fort Myers Miracle (MIN), GCL Twins, GCL Red Sox

Corpus Christi Hooks (HOU)

ROAD TO THE SHOW
DISTANCES FROM ROOKIE LEVEL TO THE MAJORS

BALTIMORE ORIOLES (From rookie level to major leagues: 1,997 miles)

ATLANTA BRAVES (2,726 miles)

WASHINGTON NATIONALS (2,735 miles)

NEW YORK YANKEES (3,656 miles)

BOSTON RED SOX (3,695 miles)

PHILADELPHIA PHILLIES (3,700 miles)

CLEVELAND INDIANS (3,703 miles)

CHICAGO WHITE SOX (White Sox have two advanced rookie teams, Bristol White Sox and Great Falls Voyagers. If a player started out at Bristol, his journey would be 1,893 miles; if he started in Great Falls, it'd be 4,004 miles)

CINCINNATI REDS (4,015 miles)

FLORIDA MARLINS (4,236 miles)

PITTSBURGH PIRATES (4,311 miles)

NEW YORK METS (4,474 miles)

DETROIT TIGERS (4,879 miles)

TAMPA BAY RAYS (4,982 miles)

MILWAUKEE BREWERS (5,261 miles)

ST. LOUIS CARDINALS (5,332 miles)

CHICAGO CUBS (5,486 miles)

MINNESOTA TWINS (5,602 miles)

KANSAS CITY ROYALS (The Royals have two advanced rookie teams. While a player would begin at AZL Royals, he could go on to Burlington Royals or Idaho Falls Chukars before advancing to Class A Burlington Bees. Via Burlington Royals: 5,820 miles; via Idaho Falls: 5,011 miles)

HOUSTON ASTROS (6,311 miles)

LOS ANGELES ANGELS OF ANAHEIM (7,466 miles)

TEXAS RANGERS (8,170 miles)

COLORADO ROCKIES (8,448 miles)

OAKLAND ATHLETICS (8,793 miles)

LOS ANGELES DODGERS (8,940 miles)

TORONTO BLUE JAYS (9,566 miles)

ARIZONA DIAMONDBACKS (9,955 miles)

SAN DIEGO PADRES (10,395 miles)

SAN FRANCISCO GIANTS (12,497 miles)

SEATTLE MARINERS (12,894 miles)

INDEPENDENT BASEBALL LEAGUES
TEAMS AND LOCATIONS 2010

Worcester Tornadoes
Brockton Rox
Bridgeport Bluefish
Long Island Ducks
Sussex Skyhawks
Newark Bears
Somerset Patriots
Camden Riversharks
Lancaster Barnstormers
York Revolution

Les Capitales de Québec

Schaumburg Flyers
Windy City ThunderBolts
Kalamazoo Kings
Oakland County Cruisers
Pittsfield Colonials
New Jersey Jackals
Lake Erie Crushers
Gary SouthShore RailCats
Washington Wild Things
Southern Maryland Blue Crabs
Florence Freedom

Traverse City Beach Bums

Lake County Fielders
Rockford RiverHawks
Joliet JackHammers
Normal CornBelters
River City Rascals
Gateway Grizzlies
Southern Illinois Miners
Evansville Otters

Pensacola Pelicans

St. Paul Saints

Winnipeg Goldeyes

Fargo-Moorhead RedHawks

Sioux Falls Canaries
Sioux City Explorers
Lincoln Saltdogs
Kansas City T-Bones
Wichita Wingnuts

Amarillo Dillas
Fort Worth Cats
Grand Prairie AirHogs
Shreveport-Bossier Captains
San Angelo Colts
Big Bend Cowboys

Edmonton Capitals

Calgary Vipers

St. George RoadRunners

Chico Outlaws

Orange County Flyers

Yuma Scorpions

Tucson Toros
West Texas Roadhogs
Las Cruces Vaqueros
El Paso Diablos
Desert Valley Mountain Lions

Laredo Broncos
Coastal Bend Thunder
Edinburg Roadrunners
Rio Grande Valley WhiteWings

Na Koa Ikaika Maui

Victoria Seals

Tijuana Cimarrones

American Association of Independent Professional Baseball - North Division
Atlantic League of Professional Baseball - Freedom Division
Canadian American Association of Professional Baseball
Frontier League - East Division
Golden Baseball League - North Division
Northern League

American Association of Independent Professional Baseball - South Division
Atlantic League of Professional Baseball - Liberty Division
Continental Baseball League
Frontier League - West Division
Golden Baseball League - South Division
United League

*West Texas Roadhogs are a travel team based in El Paso.
Desert Valley Mountain Lions are based in Van Horn, TX, but play their games in Rio Rancho, Roswell, and Taos, NM.
And if you turn the book sideways to look at this map, you can pretend to be a TV character looking at a Playboy centerfold.*

'09 WORLD BASEBALL CLASSIC
ANALYSIS OF TEAM ROSTERS

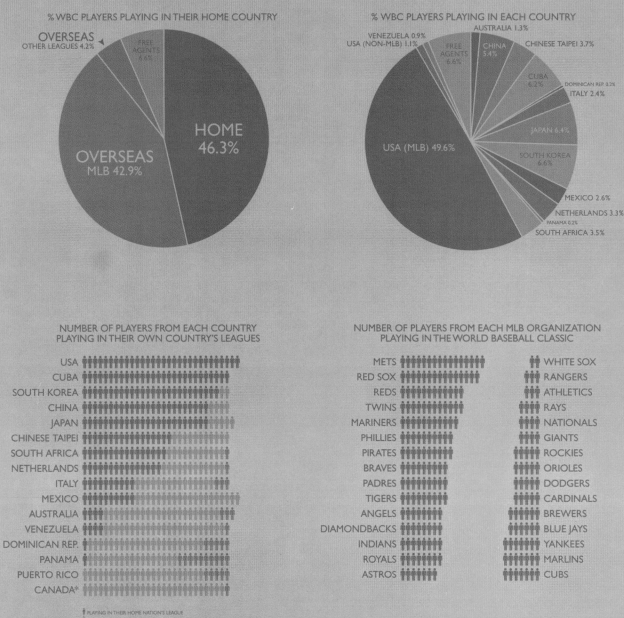

% WBC PLAYERS PLAYING IN THEIR HOME COUNTRY

OVERSEAS
OTHER LEAGUES 4.2%

FREE AGENTS 6.6%

HOME 46.3%

OVERSEAS MLB 42.9%

% WBC PLAYERS PLAYING IN EACH COUNTRY

VENEZUELA 0.9%
USA (NON-MLB) 1.1%
AUSTRALIA 1.3%
FREE AGENTS 6.6%
CHINA 5.4%
CHINESE TAIPEI 3.7%
CUBA 6.2%
DOMINICAN REP. 0.2%
ITALY 2.4%
JAPAN 6.4%
USA (MLB) 49.6%
SOUTH KOREA 6.6%
MEXICO 2.6%
NETHERLANDS 3.3%
PANAMA 0.2%
SOUTH AFRICA 3.5%

NUMBER OF PLAYERS FROM EACH COUNTRY PLAYING IN THEIR OWN COUNTRY'S LEAGUES

USA
CUBA
SOUTH KOREA
CHINA
JAPAN
CHINESE TAIPEI
SOUTH AFRICA
NETHERLANDS
ITALY
MEXICO
AUSTRALIA
VENEZUELA
DOMINICAN REP.
PANAMA
PUERTO RICO
CANADA*

PLAYING IN THEIR HOME NATION'S LEAGUE
PLAYING IN ANOTHER NATION'S LEAGUE
FREE AGENT

NUMBER OF PLAYERS FROM EACH MLB ORGANIZATION PLAYING IN THE WORLD BASEBALL CLASSIC

METS — WHITE SOX
RED SOX — RANGERS
REDS — ATHLETICS
TWINS — RAYS
MARINERS — NATIONALS
PHILLIES — GIANTS
PIRATES — ROCKIES
BRAVES — ORIOLES
PADRES — DODGERS
TIGERS — CARDINALS
ANGELS — BREWERS
DIAMONDBACKS — BLUE JAYS
INDIANS — YANKEES
ROYALS — MARLINS
ASTROS — CUBS

* FOR THE SAKE OF THIS ANALYSIS, I'VE INCLUDED THOSE WHO PLAY FOR THE TORONTO BLUE JAYS WITHIN THE UNITED STATES/MLB FIGURES. I REALIZE THAT THIS WILL ANNOY SOME OF YOU CANADIANS, AND I PROMISE, THAT ISN'T THE INTENTION. IT'S JUST THAT, THE WAY I LOOK AT IT, THEY ONLY REALLY PLAY IN CANADA BECAUSE THERE'S AN MLB FRANCHISE THERE, AND IF THAT FRANCHISE WERE IN THE STATES, THEY'D LIKELY NOT BE PLAYING IN CANADA. SORRY, Y'ALL.

KOREA BASEBALL ORGANIZATION

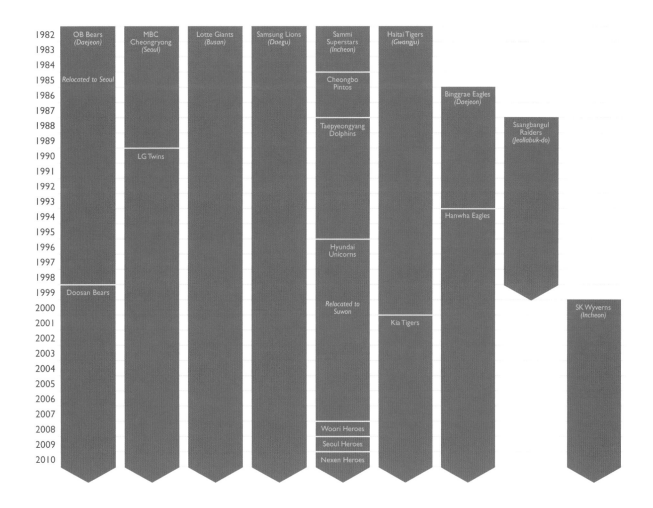

1982	OB Bears (Daejeon)	MBC Cheongryong (Seoul)	Lotte Giants (Busan)	Samsung Lions (Daegu)	Sammi Superstars (Incheon)	Haitai Tigers (Gwangju)		
1983								
1984								
1985	Relocated to Seoul				Cheongbo Pintos		Binggrae Eagles (Daejeon)	
1986								
1987								
1988					Taepyeongyang Dolphins			Ssangbangul Raiders (Jeollabuk-do)
1989								
1990		LG Twins						
1991								
1992								
1993								
1994							Hanwha Eagles	
1995								
1996					Hyundai Unicorns			
1997								
1998								
1999	Doosan Bears							
2000					Relocated to Suwon			SK Wyverns (Incheon)
2001						Kia Tigers		
2002								
2003								
2004								
2005								
2006								
2007								
2008					Woori Heroes			
2009					Seoul Heroes			
2010					Nexen Heroes			

KOREAN SERIES CHAMPIONS

TIGERS
1983, 1986, 1987, 1988, 1989, 1991, 1993, 1996, 1997, 2009

HEROES
1998, 2000, 2003, 2004

LIONS
1985, 2002, 2005, 2006

BEARS
1982, 1995, 2001

GIANTS
1984, 1992

TWINS
1990, 1994

WYVERNS
2007, 2008

EAGLES
1999

INCHEON
SK Wyverns

• SEOUL
Doosan Bears
LG Twins
Nexen Heroes

• DAEJEON
Hanwha Eagles

• DAEGU
Samsung Lions

• GWANGJU
Kia Tigers

BUSAN
Lotte Giants

JAPANESE BASEBALL HISTORY

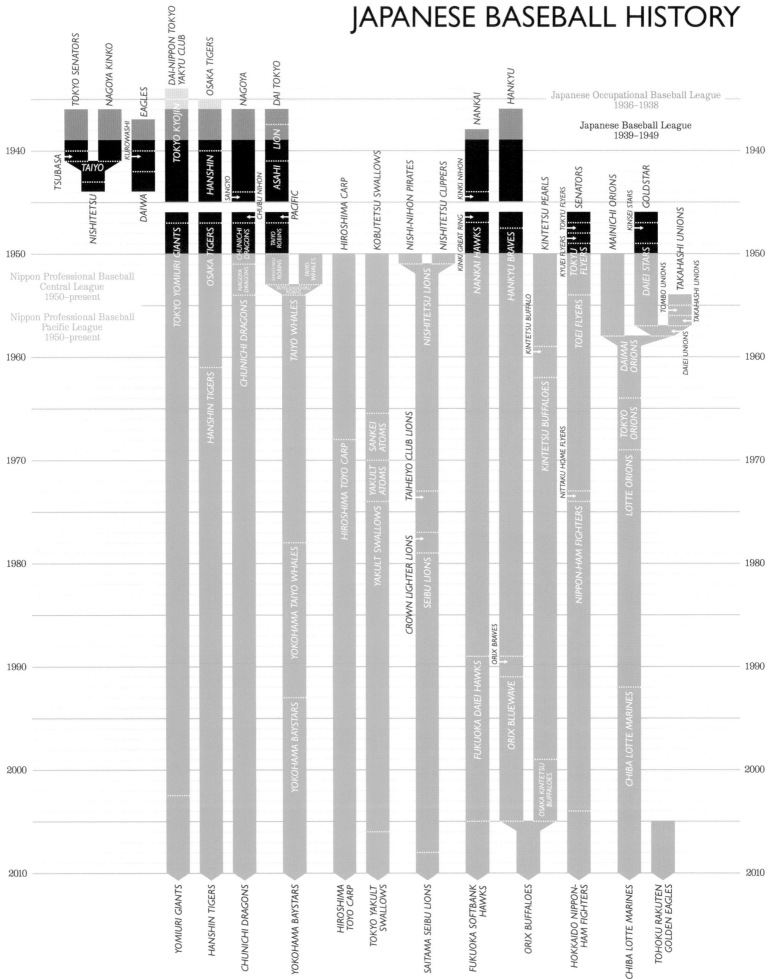

Japanese Occupational Baseball League
1936–1938

Japanese Baseball League
1939–1949

Nippon Professional Baseball
Central League
1950–present

Nippon Professional Baseball
Pacific League
1950–present

NIPPON PROFESSIONAL BASEBALL

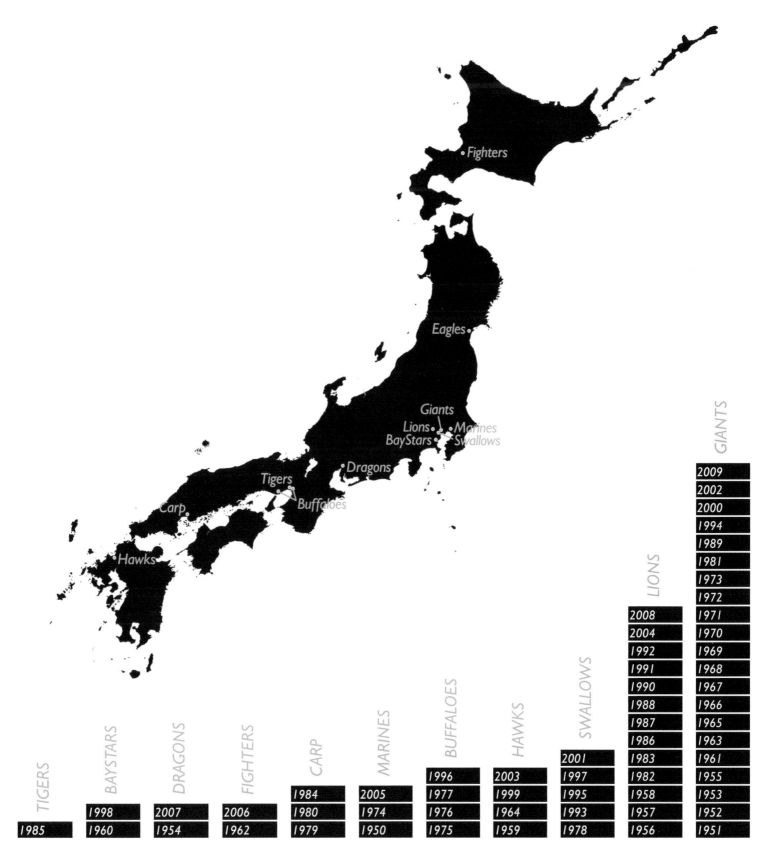

Fighters

Eagles

Giants
Lions • Marines
BayStars • Swallows

Dragons

Tigers
Carp
Buffaloes

Hawks

TIGERS	BAYSTARS	DRAGONS	FIGHTERS	CARP	MARINES	BUFFALOES	HAWKS	SWALLOWS	LIONS	GIANTS
										2009
										2002
										2000
										1994
										1989
										1981
										1973
										1972
									2008	1971
									2004	1970
									1992	1969
									1991	1968
									1990	1967
									1988	1966
									1987	1965
									1986	1963
								2001	1983	1961
							2003	1997	1982	1955
				1984		1996	1999	1995	1958	1953
	1998	2007	2006	1980	2005	1977	1964	1993	1957	1952
1985	1960	1954	1962	1979	1950	1976	1959	1978	1956	1951
						1975				

JAPAN SERIES WINNERS (BY FRANCHISE)

TAIWANESE BASEBALL

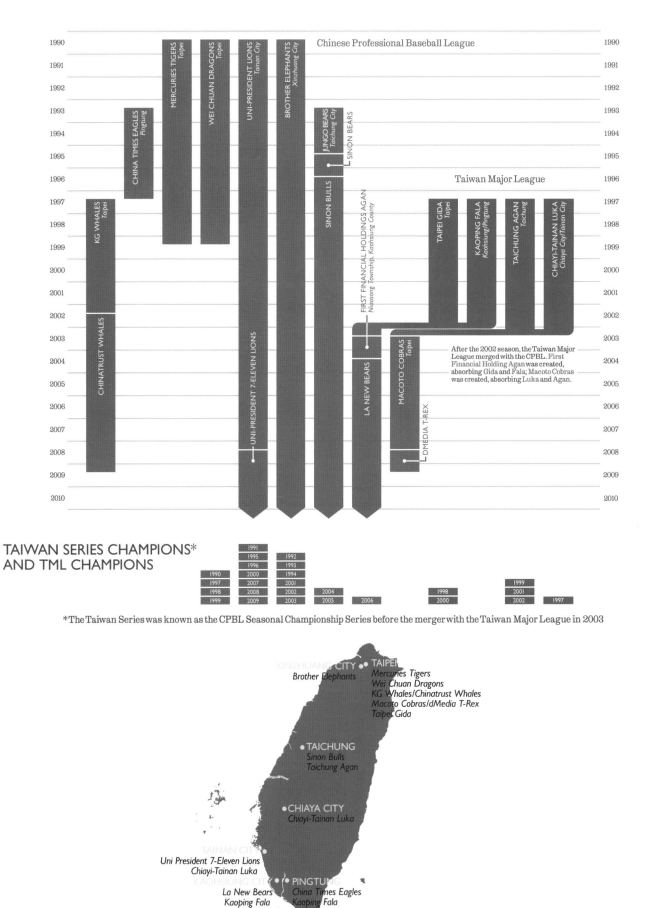

Chinese Professional Baseball League

Taiwan Major League

1990					
1991					
1992					
1993					
1994					
1995					
1996					
1997					
1998					
1999					
2000					
2001					
2002					
2003					
2004					
2005					
2006					
2007					
2008					
2009					
2010					

MERCURIES TIGERS *Taipei*
WEI CHUAN DRAGONS *Taipei*
UNI-PRESIDENT LIONS *Tainan City*
BROTHER ELEPHANTS *Xinzhuang City*
CHINA TIMES EAGLES *Pingtung*
KG WHALES *Taipei*
JUNGO BEARS *Taichung City*
SINON BEARS
SINON BULLS
CHINATRUST WHALES
UNI-PRESIDENT 7-ELEVEN LIONS
FIRST FINANCIAL HOLDINGS AGAN *Niiaosong Township, Kaohsiung County*
LA NEW BEARS
MACOTO COBRAS *Taipei*
DMEDIA T-REX
TAIPEI GIDA *Taipei*
KAOPING FALA *Kaohsiung/Pingtung*
TAICHUNG AGAN *Taichung*
CHIAYI-TAINAN LUKA *Chiaya City/Tainan City*

After the 2002 season, the Taiwan Major League merged with the CPBL. First Financial Holding Agan was created, absorbing Gida and Fala; Macoto Cobras was created, absorbing Luka and Agan.

TAIWAN SERIES CHAMPIONS* AND TML CHAMPIONS

1990	1991	1992					
1997	1995	1993				1999	
1998	1996	1994			1998	2001	
1999	2000	2001			2000	2002	1997
	2007	2002	2004				
	2008	2003	2005	2006			
	2009						

*The Taiwan Series was known as the CPBL Seasonal Championship Series before the merger with the Taiwan Major League in 2003

XINZHUANG CITY ● TAIPEI
Brother Elephants
Mercuries Tigers
Wei Chuan Dragons
KG Whales/Chinatrust Whales
Macoto Cobras/dMedia T-Rex
Taipei Gida

● TAICHUNG
Sinon Bulls
Taichung Agan

● CHIAYA CITY
Chiayi-Tainan Luka

TAINAN CITY
Uni President 7-Eleven Lions
Chiayi-Tainan Luka

KAOHSIUNG CITY ● PINGTUNG
La New Bears   China Times Eagles
Kaoping Fala   Kaoping Fala

ROAD JERSEYS
THE POWDER BLUE ERA

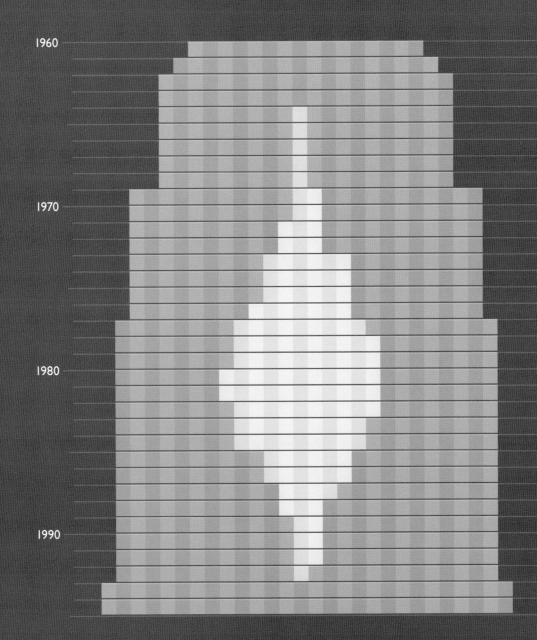

1960

1970

1980

1990

1964 (1 of 20) White Sox
1965 (1 of 20) White Sox
1966 (1 of 20) White Sox
1967 (1 of 20) White Sox
1968 (1 of 20) White Sox
1969 (2 of 24) Expos, Pilots
1970 (2 of 24) Expos, Brewers
1971 (3 of 24) Expos, Brewers, White Sox
1972 (3 of 24) Expos, Brewers, White Sox
1973 (6 of 24) Expos, Brewers, White Sox, Phillies, Royals, Twins
1974 (6 of 24) Expos, Brewers, White Sox, Phillies, Royals, Twins
1975 (6 of 24) Expos, Brewers, White Sox, Phillies, Royals, Twins
1976 (7 of 24) Expos, Brewers, Phillies, Royals, Twins, Cardinals, Rangers
1977 (9 of 26) Expos, Brewers, Phillies, Royals, Twins, Cardinals, Rangers, Blue Jays, Mariners
1978 (10 of 26) Expos, Brewers, Phillies, Royals, Twins, Cardinals, Rangers, Blue Jays, Mariners, Cubs
1979 (10 of 26) Expos, Brewers, Phillies, Royals, Twins, Cardinals, Rangers, Blue Jays, Mariners, Cubs
1980 (11 of 26) Expos, Brewers, Phillies, Royals, Twins, Cardinals, Rangers, Blue Jays, Mariners, Cubs, Braves
1981 (11 of 26) Expos, Brewers, Phillies, Royals, Twins, Cardinals, Rangers, Blue Jays, Mariners, Cubs, Braves
1982 (10 of 26) Expos, Brewers, Phillies, Royals, Twins, Cardinals, Rangers, Blue Jays, Mariners, Braves
1983 (9 of 26) Expos, Brewers, Phillies, Royals, Twins, Cardinals, Blue Jays, Mariners, Braves
1984 (9 of 26) Expos, Brewers, Phillies, Royals, Twins, Cardinals, Blue Jays, Mariners, Braves
1985 (6 of 26) Expos, Phillies, Royals, Twins, Blue Jays, Braves
1986 (6 of 26) Expos, Phillies, Royals, Twins, Blue Jays, Braves
1987 (4 of 26) Expos, Phillies, Royals, Blue Jays
1988 (3 of 26) Expos, Phillies, Royals
1989 (2 of 26) Expos, Royals
1990 (2 of 26) Expos, Royals
1991 (2 of 26) Expos, Royals
1992 (1 of 26) Expos

HIGH SOCKS
NUMBER OF PLAYERS ON OPENING DAY 2010 WEARING THEM

OF THE 284 PLAYERS WHO STARTED OPENING DAY FOR THEIR TEAMS, ONLY 22 WERE WEARING HIGH SOCKS. THAT'S 7.75%.

IN THE AMERICAN LEAGUE, 10 OF 140 WORE HIGH SOCKS.
IN THE NATIONAL LEAGUE, 12 OF 144 WORE THEM.

NEW YORK YANKEES HAD THE MOST IN THE A.L. WITH 4 OF 10.
WASHINGTON NATIONALS HAD THE MOST IN THE N.L. WITH 3 OF 9.
NO ONE WORE THEM FROM THE ANGELS, BLUE JAYS, BRAVES, BREWERS, D-BACKS, GIANTS, INDIANS, ORIOLES, PADRES, PHILLIES, RANGERS, RAYS, RED SOX, REDS, TWINS,

SIX LEFT FIELDERS WORE HIGH SOCKS, THREE PITCHERS, SHORTSTOPS, THIRD BASEMEN, CENTER FIELDERS, AND RIGHT FIELDERS WORE THEM, AND ONE DESIGNATED HITTER. NO CATCHERS, FIRST BASEMEN, OR SECOND BASEMEN WORE THEM.

17 OF THE 22 WERE AMERICAN, THREE WERE DOMINICAN, ONE WAS VENEZUELAN, AND THE OTHER WAS ICHIRO.

CAPS
YOU GOTTA LOVE A DIFFERENT-COLORED SQUATCHEE, RIGHT?

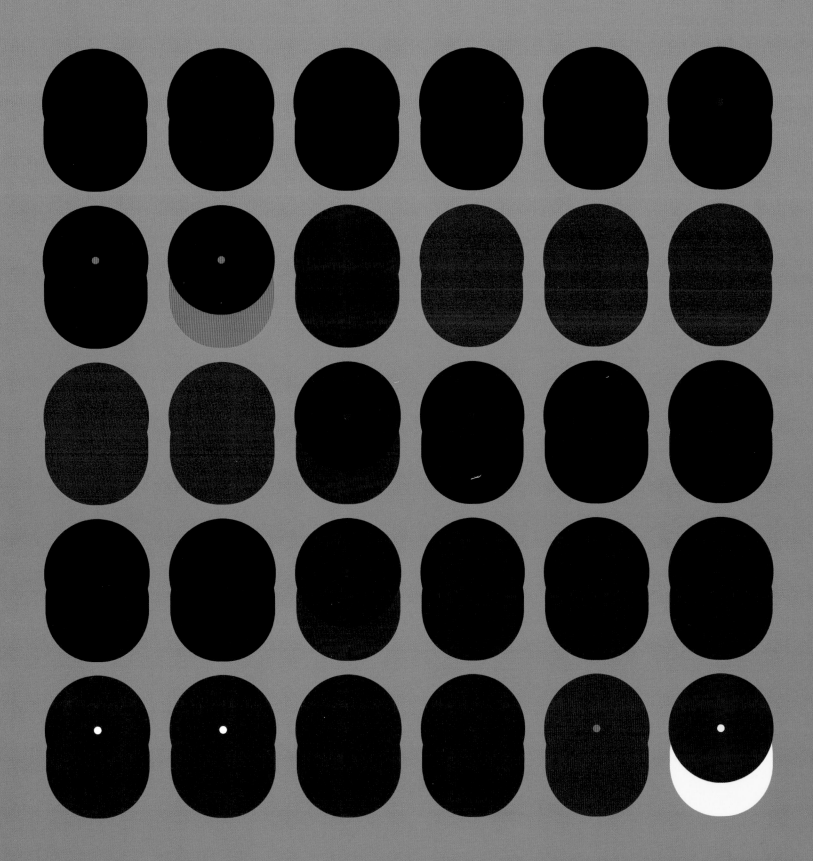

PRIMARY CAP FOR ALL THIRTY MLB TEAMS

BALL CAP STICKER REMOVAL
A HELPFUL LESSON FOR THE YOUNGSTERS

I'VE NOTICED THAT THE YOUNGER GENERATION HAS DIFFICULTY REMOVING THE STICKER FROM THE BILL. HERE'S A SIMPLE LESSON IN STICKER REMOVAL.

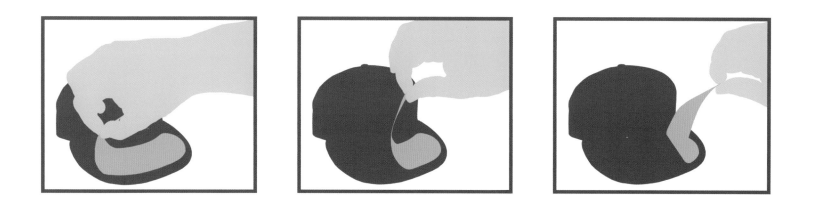

HURRAH! NOW YOUR BALL CAP IS READY TO WEAR WITHOUT ADVERTISING TO EVERYONE ON THE BUS THAT YOU'VE GOT A SIZE 7 $\frac{5}{8}$ HEAD.

BOBBLEHEAD GIVEAWAYS 2010
WHO GAVE AWAY WHAT, WHEN, AND AGAINST WHOM

Number of bobbleheads given away

current player*
former player
other

inc. Giants' Bruce Bochy bobblehead; and Mariners' Ken Griffey Jr. bobblehead that was given away 16 days after his retirement

Number of times as visiting team on bobblehead day

intra-division game
intra-league game
interleague game

Bobblehead giveaways by month

A	M	J	J	A	S	O
12	10	21	16	19	7	1

Bobblehead giveaways by day

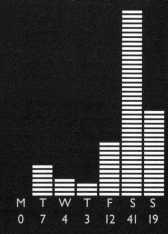

M	T	W	T	F	S	S
0	7	4	3	12	41	19

April 24 and July 31 both had five bobblehead days around the majors

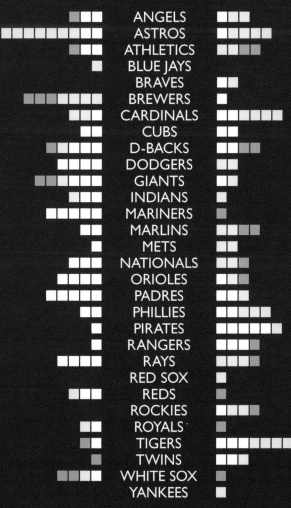

ANGELS
ASTROS
ATHLETICS
BLUE JAYS
BRAVES
BREWERS
CARDINALS
CUBS
D-BACKS
DODGERS
GIANTS
INDIANS
MARINERS
MARLINS
METS
NATIONALS
ORIOLES
PADRES
PHILLIES
PIRATES
RANGERS
RAYS
RED SOX
REDS
ROCKIES
ROYALS
TIGERS
TWINS
WHITE SOX
YANKEES

Apart from the age-specific give-aways, the Brewers, Indians, Angels, Phillies, and Pirates, gave bobbleheads to all fans. The highest number were given away by the Dodgers (50,000 each). The Marlins gave away two bobbleheads this season (Cody Ross and Chris Coghlan), but in a rather bizarre manner: they gave out 10,000 scratch cards, of which 2,500 "won" a bobblehead. Nice work, Marlins...

Bobblehead subject

OTHER*
12

FORMER PLAYER
20

CURRENT PLAYER
54

*inc. 3 Peanuts characters; 2 broadcasters; 2 "MillerLight Beer Vendor" bobbleheads; 1 stadium organist; 3 mascots/characters; and Joe DiMaggio in a SF Seals uniform, given away by the Giants. (Jerry Garcia bobblehead not included as it was part of a ticket package deal, not strictly a giveaway)

Visiting team

INTER LEAGUE
15

FROM DIVISION
30

FROM LEAGUE
41

KEVIN COSTNER
EXACTLY HOW MANY BASEBALL FILMS HAS HE STARRED IN?

4

2

27

Not including cameos or bit parts, Costner has starred in 33 films, up to and including *Swing Vote* (2008). Of those, only four have been baseball-related: *Bull Durham* (1988), *Field of Dreams* (1989), *For the Love of the Game* (1999), and *The Upside of Anger* (2005). Feels like more, doesn't it?

Two more, *American Flyers* (1985) and *Tin Cup* (1996), have also been sports-related: cycling and golf respectively. Another film, *Chasing Dreams* (1982), was also about baseball, but Costner's role is minor.

REALLY FANTASY BASEBALL
EASTERN DIVISION PENNANT TIEBREAKER GAME THAT EXISTS IN MY HEAD

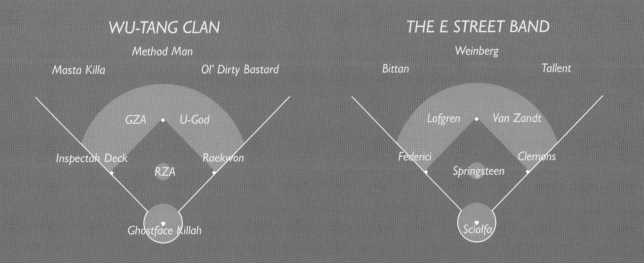

WU-TANG CLAN

Method Man

Masta Killa   Ol' Dirty Bastard

GZA   U-God

Inspectah Deck   Raekwon

RZA

Ghostface Killah

THE E STREET BAND

Weinberg

Bittan   Tallent

Lofgren   Van Zandt

Federici   Clemons

Springsteen

Scialfa

A tiebreaker game in the Eastern Division to determine who will go on to play Earth, Wind & Fire in the Championship Series.

	1	2	3	4	5	6	7	8	9	R	H	E
WU-TANG CLAN	1	0	0	1	0	0	0	1	1	4	11	1
E STREET BAND	0	0	0	0	1	0	2	0	0	3	7	0

	AB	R	H	RBI	BB	SO	LOB	AVG
U-God, 2B	5	0	2	0	0	0	1	.400
Masta Killa, LF	4	2	2	1	1	0	0	.500
GZA/Genius, SS	5	0	1	0	0	1	0	.200
Raekwon, 1B	4	0	0	0	1	0	4	.000
Method Man, CF	4	1	3	1	1	0	0	.750
Ol' Dirty Bastard, RF	3	0	1	1	1	1	2	.333
Inspectah Deck, 3B	3	1	1	0	0	1	0	.333
Ghostface Killah, C	3	0	1	0	1	1	0	.333
RZA, P	4	0	0	0	0	2	1	.000
	35	4	11	4	5	6	9	

	AB	R	H	RBI	BB	SO	LOB	AVG
Nils Lofgren, SS	4	0	1	0	0	1	2	.250
Steven Van Zandt, 2B	4	0	1	0	0	0	0	.250
Max Weinberg, CF	4	0	0	0	0	0	0	.000
Clarence Clemons, 1B	4	1	1	1	0	1	0	.250
Garry Tallent, RF	4	0	0	0	0	1	1	.000
Roy Bittan, LF	4	0	0	0	1	0	0	.000
Danny Federici, 3B	3	1	2	0	1	1	1	.667
Patti Scialfa, C	4	0	1	0	0	0	1	.250
Bruce Springsteen, P	4	0	1	2	0	1	1	.250
	35	3	7	3	1	6	6	

	IP	H	R	ER	BB	SO	HR	ERA
RZA (W, 1-0)	9.0	7	3	2	1	6	1	3.00

	IP	H	R	ER	BB	SO	HR	ERA
Springsteen (L, 0-1)	9.0	11	4	4	5	6	1	4.00

BATTING
2B Man
HR Killa
RBI Killa 2, Man, Bastard
GIDP RZA, Deck, Bastard

BASERUNNING
SB U-God, Killa

FIELDING
DP GZA-U-God-Raekwon
E Bastard

BATTING
2B Van Zandt
HR Clemons
RBI Springsteen 2, Clemons
GIDP Van Zandt

FIELDING
DP Van Zandt-Lofgren-Clemons, Federici-Van Zandt-Clemons, Lofgren-Van Zandt-Clemons

Umpires HP J. Bonham 1B J. Page 2B R. Plant 3B J.P. Jones
Venue Asbury Park, NJ
Weather 73 degrees, clear
Wind 8mph, R to L
Time 2:56
Attendance 28,146

FINAL STANDINGS
EASTERN DIVISION

	W	L	Pct.
Wu-Tang	12	6	.667
E Street	12	6	.667
Kool Gang	9	9	.500
Pogues	3	15	.167

WESTERN DIVISION

	W	L	Pct.
Earth WF	13	5	.722
Chicago	10	8	.556
Slipknot	9	9	.500
Poly Spree	4	14	.222

CHAMPIONSHIP SERIES

EARTH, WIND & FIRE vs.
WU-TANG CLAN

Oct 9 at Boogie Wonderland Park
Oct 10 at Boogie Wonderland Park
Oct 12 at Shaolin Field
Oct 13 at Shaolin Field
* Oct 14 at Shaolin Field
* Oct 16 at Boogie Wonderland Park
* Oct 17 at Boogie Wonderland Park
* if needed

NOTES ON THE SOURCES

Unless otherwise noted, all data is from Baseball-Reference.com.

Front Cover: The top hundred books on Amazon.com when searching for the term "baseball"

Pro Baseball History: Baseball-Reference.com, MLB.com, Wikipedia.org

Relocations: Baseball-Reference.com, MLB.com, Wikipedia.org

Team Names: MLB.com, Wikipedia.org, SportsEncyclopedia.com

After Jackie: MLB.com

Number 42: Baseball-Reference.com, MLB.com, Wikipedia.org

Retired Numbers: MLB.com, Wikipedia.org

Yankees' Retired Numbers: Baseball-Reference.com, MLB.com, Wikipedia.org

Hall of Fame: BaseballHallofFame.org, MLB.com, Wikipedia.org, *Cooperstown Confidential* by Zev Chafets (New York: Bloomsbury, 2009)

Home Runs & PEDs: Baseball-Reference.com, BaseballsSteroidEra.com, mlb.com/mlb/ news/mitchell/index.jsp (Links to Mitchell Report PDF)

1998 Home Run Chase: Baseball-Reference.com, www.nytimes .com/2009/07/05/sports/baseball/05homers.html

Barry Bonds' Walks: Baseball-Reference.com, Earth.Google.com

MLB Fields: Maps.Google.com, MLB.com

MLB Ballparks: MLB.com, Wikipedia.org, AndrewClem.com/ Baseball, BallparksOfBaseball.com

Green Monster: MLB.com, Wikipedia.org, NFL.com

Diamonds in Manhattan: Maps.Google.com, Baseball-Reference.com

Parking Lots: Maps.Google.com

Night Games: Baseball-Almanac.com, Wikipedia.org

Nearest Field: Earth.Google.com

Four-Sport Cities: Wikipedia.org

2009 Attendance: MLB.com

Dugouts: MLB.TV, Flickr.com

Ballpark Orientations: Earth.Google.com

Smoking: Personal experience from visits to ballparks in 2008 and 2009, each team's ballpark guide at mlb.com

Ballpark Elevations: Stadium altitudes listed on Sony Computer Entertainment's "MLB 09: The Show" for PlayStation Portable

Turner, Montana: Earth.Google.com, Maps.Google.com

Google Street View Screenshots: Maps.Google.com

Perfect Games: Baseball-Reference.com, Wikipedia.org

Don't Mention It: MLB.TV

Total Pitches: MLB.com, Earth.Google.com

Lefties, Righties, & Switchies: MLB.com

Baserunning: MLB.com

Stolen Bases: MLB.com, Modells.com, LawInfoBoulder.com

200,000 Baseballs: Maps.Google.com, www.NYDailyNews.com/ sports/baseball/2010/06/15/2010-06-15_having_a_ball.html

Arizona: MLB.com, GoldenBaseball.com, Pointstreak.com, Examiner.com, OuSportsCentral.com, AZHardball.com

Homosexuality: MLB.com, Wikipedia.org, OutSports.com/ baseball/ 2003/0617glennburke.htm

Biggest Payroll: Baseball-Reference.com, baseballsalaries. usatoday.com

Payroll: baseballsalaries.usatoday.com

New York Post: NYPost.com/archives/covers

Interleague Play: Baseball-Reference.com, MLB.com

Nolan Ryan: Baseball-Reference.com, Wikipedia.org

Nolan Ryan or Two 8–7 Pitchers: Baseball-Reference.com, Wikipedia.org

Roger Clemens: Baseball-Reference.com, Wikipedia.org, *The Rocket That Fell to Earth: Roger Clemens and the Rage for Baseball Immortality* by Jeff Pearlman (New York: HarperCollins, 2009)

John 3:16: Baseball-Reference.com, Wikipedia.org

Bradenia: Maps.Google.com

A-Rod's Salary: mlbcontracts.blogspot.com, Wikipedia.org

Centaur: MLB.com

Mike Morgan/Matt Stairs: Baseball-Reference.com, TheBaseballCube.com, Wikipedia.org

Ted Williams: RetroSheet.org

"Rock'n Me": Baseball-Reference.com, TheBaseballCube.com

Tigers: Baseball-Reference.com, UMM.edu/sleep/normal_sleep .htm, BLS.gov/news.release/atus.nr0.htm, JoePosnanski.com/ JoeBlog/2010/04/12/time-of-game/. After reading Posnanski's blog post about the length of games, I got to wondering how much time a very dedicated fan would spend watching their team. As Joe listed the five fastest playing teams and the five slowest playing teams in the American League, I decided to research one of the teams he didn't mention—thus the Tigers.

Washington DC: Baseball-Reference.com, Wikipedia.org

Kansas City: MLB.com, Baseball-Reference.com

Cleveland Indians: http://factfinder.census.gov The U.S. Census Bureau's American Community Survey Demographic and Housing Estimates 2005–2007.

"O Canada": MLB.com, Baseball-Reference.com, twitter.com/ Montreal_Expos

Montreal Expos: Baseball-Reference.com, Wikipedia.org, http:// assets.espn.go.com/mlb/news/2002/0205/1323166.html, http:// assets.espn.go.com/mlb/s/2002/0205/1323230.html

SkyDome Cost: Baseball-Reference.com, Wikipedia.org

All-American Girls League: Baseball-Reference.com, Wikipedia.org

Pacific Coast League: Baseball-Reference.com, Wikipedia.org

Minor Leagues: MinorLeagueBaseball.com, Baseball-Reference .com, Wikipedia.org

Road to the Majors: MinorLeagueBaseball.com, Baseball-Reference.com, Wikipedia.org, Maps.Google.com

Independent Leagues: Baseball-Reference.com, Wikipedia.org, AmericanAssociationbaseball.com, AtlanticLeague.com, CanAmLeague.com, CBLProBall.com, FrontierLeague.com, GoldenBaseball.com, NorthernLeague.com, UnitedLeague.org

World Baseball Classic: Baseball-Reference.com, Wikipedia.org, WorldBaseballClassic.com

Korean Baseball: Baseball-Reference.com, Wikipedia.org, BaseballGuru.com, KoreaBaseball.com, MyWorldOfBaseball .com, Maps.Google.com

Japanese Baseball: Baseball-Reference.com, Wikipedia.org, JapaneseBaseball.com, JapanBall.com, JapanBaseballDaily.com, BaseballGuru.com, www2.gol.com/users/jallen/jimball.html

Taiwanese Baseball: Baseball-Reference.com, Wikipedia.org, BaseballGuru.com, taiwanbaseball.blogspot.com, Maps.Google .com

Powder Blues: http://exhibits.baseballhalloffame.org/dressed_ to_the_nines

High Socks: MLB.TV

Caps: MLB.com

Bobbleheads: Amazon.com

Kevin Costner: IMDB.com, Wikipedia.org

ACKNOWLEDGMENTS

Biggest thanks of all go to Pete Beatty who made the process of putting this book together such a joy.

Thanks to Farley Chase for getting the ball rolling.

Further thanks to Barbara and Kraig Bartel, John Bassett, Amy Baumberger, Kevin Braddock, Torben Brown, Dana Constance, Rebecca Cook, Tommy Craggs at Deadspin, Taryn Diamond, Sean Forman and all at Baseball-Reference.com, Walt and Jenny Frazer, Laura Griffin, Lowell Heppner, Mark Hooper, Lisa Howard, Jeff Iezzi, Scott Ingram, Ben Kabak, Joe Pawlikowski, and Mike Axisa at RiverAvenueBlues.com, Nate Knaebel, Sacha Lambert, Mark Leonard, Heather Mathews, Elliot Mealia, Jim McDonough, Jim Meyers, Keith McColl, Jackie McGeown, Steve McLay, Michael Moineau, Juliana Mundim, Rob Neyer, Eric Nusbaum and Ted Walker at PitchersandPoets .com, Michael O'Connor, Andrew Otwell, Hanni Pannier, Justin Parker, Derick Rhodes, Josh Rosen, Joe Ross, everyone at Squirly's, Ashley Schaefer, Andrew Stoeten at DrunkJaysFans.com, Mark Svartz, Elizabeth Van Itallie, Claire Walton, and every person I've chatted with at a game, in a bar, by email, on Twitter . . . thanks for making a foreigner welcome in your sport's world.

A NOTE ON THE AUTHOR

Craig Robinson is a English artist, illustrator, and writer. Robinson runs the websites www.flipflopflyin.com and www.flipflopflyball.com, blogs at www.flipflopflyin.com, and has published three books: *Minipops, Fun Fun Fun,* and *Atlas, Schmatlas.*

He is a New York Yankees fan with a soft spot for the Colorado Rockies and a man crush on Ichiro. His last team was the Prenzlauer Berg Piranhas of the Berlin Mixed Softball League (.452 /.575 /.548, defensively weak).